The Cognitive Behavioral Therapy Workbook:

Discover a Simple Method to Overcome Anxiety, Depression, Eating Disorders, Social Phobia and Begin Your Journey to Healing

2024

Table of Contents

Introduction 5

Chapter 1 16
UNDERSTANDING YOUR STATE OF MIND 16
  Identifying feelings 17
  Diving into the world of emotions 22
  Types of emotions 23
  Where emotions "grow" from 24
  How emotions affect us..25
  How to get your emotions under control 26
  Visualizing the future 27
  How to develop the power of visualization 28
  Exercise "My delightful life in 1 year." 30
  A letter to you in the future..34

Chapter 2 36
CHECK YOUR ANXIETY LEVEL..36
  Definition of anxiety 37
  What is anxiety? 37
  Symptoms of anxiety 38
  Causes of Anxiety 38
  Peculiarities of family upbringing 39
  Post-traumatic stress 39
  Intrapersonal sources of anxiety..40
  Types of Anxiety. 41
  Diagnosing an Anxiety Condition. 42
  12 simple ways to calm down and not get stressed out 47
  6 effective grounding exercises for anxiety and intense emotions 51
  Treatment of anxiety disorders 55

Chapter 3 59
MAYBE I'M DEPRESSED. 59
  Definition of depression 60
  Causes of depression 61
  Classification of depression 64
  Forms of depression by type of course: 65
  Symptoms of depression 69

Symptoms of depression by age 71

Diagnosis of depression 73

Which doctor to see if you suspect depression 74

Tests and questionnaires to detect depression 74

Signs of depression: 74

The Beck Depression Scale test. 75

Treatment of depression 79

    Antidepressants 80

    Instrumental methods of treatment 82

Cognitive behavioral therapy for depression 83

How CPT sessions work in the treatment of depression 85

Prevention of depression 87

Chapter 4 89

EATING DISORDERS 89

Types of eating disorders 91

    Anorexia 91

    Bulimia 93

    Rumination 95

    Compulsive overeating 95

    Emotional drinking 97

    Orthorexia 99

    Night eating syndrome 99

Causes and symptoms of eating disorders 100

    There are three broad groups of eating disorders: 100

    Symptoms. How do you know if a person has an eating disorder? 102

    Symptoms that may manifest: 103

    Signs of a Covert Eating Disorder: 103

    Causes of eating disorder development 104

Complications of an eating disorder 105

Diagnosis of an eating disorder 106

Tests to detect signs of an eating disorder 107

Eating Attitudes Test (EAT) 107

Dutch Eating Behavior Questionnaire (DEBQ) 111

Eating disorder treatment 115

    Psychotherapy for eating disorders 116

    Cognitive-behavioral therapy exercises 117

Emotion Diary : 122

Eating disorder prevention.. 123

Chapter 5 124

SOCIAL ANXIETY DISORDER 124

The concept of Social phobia 125

Stages and forms of the disease 127

Signs of Social phobia 129

Causes of social phobia 130

Diagnosis 131

Liebowitz Social Anxiety Scale testing 132

Treatment 134

Drug therapy 135

Psychotherapy 135

Techniques for CBT work with social phobia 136

The second method is Distancing. 137

Prevention 140

Conclusion 142

References 143

A Special Gift for You, Dear Reader!.. 147

Introduction
Be sure to read before you begin

I drew inspiration for writing this book from my own experience. For many years, struggling with prolonged depression and anxiety disorders, having tried many different methods, and working with different specialists, I was able to get out of the abyss of sadness. I was able to return to a normal life that I had never dreamed of. At some point of despair, you think that such a state is the norm, but looking around, you find only confirmation that everyone lives like that.

At a certain stage of my life, while undergoing another training in search of a healing resource, I was fortunate to be introduced to the approaches of cognitive-behavioral therapy. In just a few years, I was able to vein to a normal life, to feel like a normal and happy person for no reason.

Now I want to tell as many people on the planet about it as possible. I would like to share the knowledge that I have gathered from various sources, which may be useful to one more person. Even if at least one person after reading this book finds support and an idea for healing, it will be the highest reward for me.

Okay, let's stop with the lyrics and get down to business. Let's look at what cognitive-behavioral therapy is and what the advantages of this methodology are.

Cognitive-behavioral therapy was created in the mid-20th century by two prominent psychologists from the United States - Albert Ellis and Aaron Beck. The main ideas of this direction of psychotherapy, which distinguished it from others, were the thorough scientific substantiation of all the practices used and the emphasis on working with the patient's thinking.

As a result, the technique proved to be so versatile and successful that it quickly spread around the world. Many practitioners and scientists began to use cognitive behavioral therapy widely, making it the most widespread and effective form of psychotherapy within a few decades. Today, cognitive behavioral therapy is the method of first choice in most cases.

The main advantage of cognitive-behavioral therapy is its universality. For many pathological conditions, including obsessive-compulsive, generalized anxiety, and panic disorder, there is simply no alternative to cognitive-behavioral therapy. Any other methodology is much less effective, time-consuming, or has no effect at all.

Another advantage of cognitive behavioral therapy is the constant improvement of the method. This is made possible by advances in neurobiology. Every year, scientists learn more and more about how the human brain is organized, which pushes cognitive sciences forward. All theoretical scientific advances are quickly transformed for practical application.

So how was this approach born and what is its history?

Future psychologist Aaron Temkin Beck was born in July 1921 in the American city of Providence. Three years before his birth, his older sister died of influenza, which was a great blow to his mother, so Aaron's childhood was spent in the atmosphere of her severe depression.

Beck himself was a shy and withdrawn child, often sick and hospitalized. Once he received a serious injury to his arm, and the treatment led to the fact that he became haunted by phobias, panic fear of getting new injuries, and fear of bleeding. It was this circumstance that predetermined his choice of profession.

In 1946, he entered Yale University School of Medicine, where he specialized in neurology, but then went into psychiatry and began studying psychoanalysis.

At first, Beck was convinced that psychoanalysis was the only system that could help a person deal with mental problems. By the late 1950s, however, he had concluded that Freudian psychoanalysis was not as effective. In particular, psychoanalysts believed that depression was the result of anger turned inward, however, the psychologist noticed that depressed patients did not feel angry, but rather just considered themselves failures (here, we can see a very simplified understanding of aggression in the concept of depth therapy).

Beck found that it's these kinds of assumptions, and the "automatic thoughts" associated with them, along the lines of "I'm always unlucky," "I've always been unsociable," that are the root of all problems.

From there, he decided that transforming thinking was to help patients correct their disorder. He began encouraging patients to focus on negative beliefs in their daily lives rather than conflicts from childhood, and he invited people to disprove their assumptions, test them in their lives, and gather evidence that supported the positive alternative.

This practice contributed to the improvement of patients' condition. This is how cognitive psychotherapy was born.

The discovery that their thinking determines the state of depressed patients led Aaron Beck to the idea that, first, our emotional and behavioral reactions are determined by our thinking, and second, that other mental disorders can be interpreted in the same way. Thus, the ABC formula of cognitive therapy, which we will talk about.

To explain why people, have certain maladaptive thoughts, Aaron Beck expanded his scheme not only horizontally but also vertically, saying that our deep-seated beliefs determine certain maladaptive thoughts.

Aaron Beck argued that our underlying beliefs distort our automatic thoughts. All of these beliefs have three vectors: about us, about others, and the world.

In doing so, Beck, in the course of his practice, first identified two categories of underlying beliefs and then added a third.

1. **Worthlessness**. The first group of underlying beliefs are beliefs about one's worthlessness. These beliefs usually sound like "I am worthless" and are built on assumptions about activity along the lines of "If I don't do something perfectly or achieve something, then I am worthless myself."
2. **Unattractiveness**. The second group of beliefs is "I am unattractive" and is related to relationships with people based on the assumption "If I don't please people, they will reject me".
3. **Helplessness**. The third group of beliefs sounds like "I am helpless", it is based on the assumption "If I don't control everything, something terrible will happen and I won't be able to handle it".

All these beliefs can be described along the three vectors mentioned earlier, that is, as beliefs about oneself, about others, and the world. For example, the helplessness belief can be described as "I am helpless, and others and the world in general are dangerous.

According to Beck, we can put all maladaptive thoughts into these categories in one way or another. For example, the thought "I'm dying" in a panic attack can be attributed to helplessness, and the thought "They're laughing at me" to unattractiveness.

It is also interesting that this model is a direct reflection of psychoanalysis' idea of the individual's desire to compensate for these beliefs. Thus, CBT also considers several strategies by which an individual seeks to compensate for these beliefs.

1. **Worthlessness - Perfectionism.** Worthlessness is compensated for by perfectionism, the individual tends to set himself exaggerated goals and wants to increase his productivity so as not to face his worthlessness. Hence distortions arise when a person devalues the results of his work, for example, saying that he could have done better.

2. **Unattractiveness - Conformism.** In one's unattractiveness, a person seeks to compensate for conformism, constantly adjusting to other people and paying excessive attention to the social environment, hence there are all sorts of thoughts that someone is mocking or about their loneliness.

3. **Helplessness - Hyper control.** Helplessness is compensated for by hyper control when the individual is unable to let go of the lever of control (this, by the way, is one of the main problems with hypnotization). It is with this compensation that catastrophizing often occurs, in the style of "I have no control over what happens to me, which means something terrible is going to happen".

As long as the compensatory mechanisms are more or less working, the person still feels comfortable, however, as soon as the ideal picture is violated he experiences frustration.

The second provision of CPT, related to deep beliefs, also reflects the ideas of psychoanalysis. In particular, it is assumed that deep-seated beliefs change little during life and are almost impossible to change with the help of psychotherapy, and, incidentally, they are largely associated with various borderline disorders.

Deep-seated beliefs are rigid and seek self-affirmation, and therefore utilize cognitive distortions, twisting our perceptions and thoughts.

Cognitive distortions

Cognitive-behavioral therapy explores, among other things, how underlying beliefs are related to our thoughts, and it is cognitive distortions that connect them. The lists of cognitive distortions in cognitive therapy differ from those offered in cognitive psychology, and there are many lists, so I will give you the classification that seems to be the most adequate.

1. **Selective filtering** focuses on the negative aspects of a situation and devalues the positive ones. For example, a client may say: "I was promoted and now I have to work twice as much", without noticing that he or she will be paid twice as much.

2. **Black-and-white thinking** is viewing the world in exclusively polar values of "all or nothing", without the possibility of seeing intermediate options. Thus, a person thinks, "Either I pass the entrance exam, or I will forever remain poor and unemployed" or "Either we never quarrel, or we break off the relationship".

3. **Overgeneralization** - formulating global conclusions based on single events and cases, without taking into account the whole possible sample of situations. For example, a man may claim that he cannot find a girlfriend simply because his two attempts to do so have failed.

4. **Exaggeration** - exaggerating the complexity and magnitude of the problem situation. For example, a client may state, "My public speaking was an absolute nightmare" or "My disorder prevents me from living a normal life.

5. **Negative predictions** are unreasonable forecasting of a negative version of events without taking into account the probabilities of other outcomes. For example, a client may say to a therapist, "You can't help me anyway," or a person may assume before any exam or competition that he or she will fail.

6. **Catastrophizing** is an excessive exaggeration of the negative significance of an event. Thus, while in the previous case, we were talking about a possible real outcome, here we are more likely to talk about what this outcome could lead to. For example, "If I have another panic attack I will die" or "If she leaves me I will be alone forever".

7. **Low frustration tolerance** - believing in one's inability to cope with negative states and exaggerating their significance. For example, a client may say that he or she is unable to cope with his or her anxiety or a fight with his or her partner.

8. **Labeling** - implies a global assessment of a personality based on its manifestations. For example, a client may say, "Well, you're just a psychologist, you only care about money" or "He's a typical dork and can't understand me.

9. **Mind-reading** - making baseless assumptions about what other people think about a person, as well as believing that others must know their thoughts. For example, a woman may claim to give men obvious hints and they still don't approach her for some reason, or a man may claim to know how his mother-in-law hates him.

10. **Painful comparison** - involves comparing oneself to other people, when only based on a particular area a general conclusion is made. For example, a client may say, "I am worthless because other people my age already have families and children" or "Most people I know earn more than me, which means I have achieved nothing.

11. **Debt** - making unreasonable demands on oneself, others, and the world. The distortion is often formed from parental attitudes and may sound like "A man must give his duty to his country" or "A man must provide for his family" or "People are obliged to show empathy".

12. **Emotional reasoning** - elevating an assumption to reality based on its emotional significance. For example: "I go to a healer and get well because I feel better with each session" or "This situation will be bad because I will feel bad in it".

13. **Personalization** - believing that you are the cause of other people's behavior and everything that happens around you. For example, "If I hadn't behaved like that, she wouldn't have left me" or "If I had helped her then, she would still be alive".

14. **Magical thinking** is the belief that a person can influence others and events in the world in an indirect way contrary to cause-and-effect relationships. For example, "I think I set him up with my thoughts" or "I will teach you to attract money to yourself" or "I got rid of my diseases with the help of orgone energy and can treat others with it".

Cognitive-behavioral psychotherapy is notable for its formalized nature and, therefore, each time follows the same algorithm consisting of several stages.

1. **Status Review**. In the first step, the therapist reviews the client's current state and invites the client to share the events of the past week, which helps, on the one hand, to set a new agenda and, on the other hand, to identify difficulties that may have arisen in completing homework. Forms for such a status review will be provided in this book.

2. **Repetition**. The second stage involves repeating the findings of the previous session or all past work. The client's successes are noted. This ensures continuity of knowledge as well as reinforcing client loyalty.

3. **Agenda**. The agenda is then set and this can usually be done in conjunction with the therapist, either based on current life circumstances or the targets of influence identified in past sessions.

4. **Discussion of the problem**. Next, the work phase itself begins. Here, either the client's problem is discussed, or the client is shown new techniques that he or she will later perform on his or her own. Many techniques can be found on the pages of this book.

5. **Homework**. In the fifth stage, the client is given a new homework assignment based on what was done in the session.

6. **Summarizing**. The session ends with a summary of what was accomplished in the session.

This whole process takes about 40 minutes, while the session itself and the execution of the techniques in it last about 15-20 minutes. The therapist acts as a coach or teacher who provides the client with the tools and techniques he or she needs. Of course, there is no in-depth contact as in other types of therapy, but there is no need for it.

In essence, cognitive behavioral therapy is a symptom-centered approach where the therapist pushes back specifically on the symptom.

Depending on the symptom, different protocols are used. Thus, one can find protocols for the treatment of insomnia, depression, panic disorder, borderline disorder, etc., which are a fixed sequence of steps of separate diagnostic and therapeutic techniques. For example, in the case of anxiety-phobic disorders, an exposure therapy technique will be used, in the case of depression a diary of successes and achievements will be used, and in the case of stress and insomnia a progressive relaxation technique will be used.

In this sense, CBT has a great advantage over other therapies, such as psychoanalysis, where despite the great classifications and theories, the technique for any disorder, problem, or inner conflict remains roughly the same.

Since CBT is also a technique-centered approach, there is a huge number of techniques in it, and today there are so many of them that probably no cognitive therapist would be able to list them, let alone perform them competently. I am also unlikely to be able to give you the entire list of modern techniques, as well as the entire list of Aaron Beck's classic techniques, so let us consider only the main ones.

One such technique, diaries, is aimed at identifying automatic thoughts. The first thing the client is offered to do is to keep an ABC diary. In this diary, the client writes down situations - thoughts - and reactions by the ABC scheme, thus learning to independently identify his/her thoughts and concretize his/her request.

Diary keeping occurs throughout the psychotherapy process, and during the sessions themselves, the therapist continually helps the client to identify their maladaptive cognitions and then demonstrates how to write them in the diary.

Since the client is often unable to label the disturbing thought, the therapist uses additional techniques to identify it. For example, the therapist uses a fill-in-the-blank technique, filling in only the event and reaction columns in the diary, and leaving a blank in the thought column so that the client can think about what could be put there.

The therapist can ask, "What would another person or a friend think in your place?" to elicit the thought. The therapist may suggest replaying the problematic situation so that it is easier for the client to reproduce the problematic thought.

In addition, a differentiation technique is used, where a column is added to the table with a division into fact or opinion. In this way, the client learns to distinguish between factual descriptions of events and distorted interpretations of them.

Eventually, when the client learns to identify his/her thoughts, he/she and the therapist fill in more complex tables. This is how a stress diary is used, in which the client notes generalized situations and reactions rather than specific ones. Such a diary allows for the identification of deeper distortions and beliefs, which are also later entered into an expanded ABC diary.

Then come the techniques of challenging thoughts and here, first of all, we are talking about Socratic dialog, which has nothing in common with the dialogs that Socrates himself conducted, except for the idea that we bring the person to the thought we need with our questions.

The technique of Socratic dialog is reduced to the fact that the therapist first asks himself why the client's thought is wrong, and having given himself the answer, he comes up with a corresponding question for the client. For example, the client states that during his speech someone in the audience laughed, which means that they laughed at him. From here, the therapist asks himself first: "Why might this thought be wrong?" and concludes that, for example, "The person might not have laughed at the client, but at something else."

Consequently, you can ask the client, "Could there be any other reasons for that person's laughter?" or "Could it be that they weren't laughing at you, but at a joke that was sent to them on social media during the show."

Gradually, the client himself learns to challenge his thoughts in this way and expands his ABC diary, now not only listing irrational thoughts and beliefs but also rational responses to them.

Pro and con arguments. Here, a table is drawn where the arguments "for" and "against" a given thought or belief are labeled in different columns and sometimes given weights. The idea is to show the client that his dysfunctional judgment is simply not beneficial to him.

Behavioral experiment. This technique involves asking the client to test a thought. For example, if he thinks that everyone will laugh at him at a speech, we might suggest that he speak up. In most cases, certain thoughts are disproved, or their consequences are disproved because the individual is most often afraid not of the facts, but of their outcomes. For example, a person might be afraid that if he or she is laughed at a performance, he or she will die of shame, but when he or she is laughed at, he or she realizes that it doesn't mean anything and calms down.

Decatastrophization. Separately, the technique of decatastrophizing is used for catastrophizing assumptions. This technique assumes that we develop the sequence of events on which the individual stops when catastrophizing. For example, a girl states that if she stands up for her opinion to a guy, the guy will dump her. Then we ask, "What happens next?" - "What happens next is I'll feel bad and I'll cry." - "What happens next?" - "Well I will be alone, I will be lonely" - "Well, a month, two, a year will pass, what will happen next?", - "Well I think by then I will have found someone new". Thus, the client realizes that the situation is not so catastrophic and that it does not end with breaking up with the boyfriend.

Reframing. Reframing involves replacing a client's inadequate thought with a more rational and adaptive thought that implies a specific behavior. For example, if a client states that "He will never be able to start a family" we can reframe this into the thought "If I don't try, I definitely won't succeed, but if I try to get to know someone, I will at least have a chance".

Decentering. The technique involves asking the client to accept their problem and then simply shift their attention to something else. For example, a client might accept his or her anxiety: "Yes, I have anxiety, and I'm probably going to have a panic attack soon, but there's nothing I can do about it, so I'll just distract myself with my stuff. An example of this technique is counting to yourself during a panic attack.

Back in the Past. CBT also uses the technique of "Back to the Past", where we ask the client to describe a situation from the perspective of an objective observer. For example, if the client feels that he or she made a laughing stock of him or herself when he or she slipped on the ice, then from a third-person perspective, he or she may take it more coolly: "Well, yes, it was funny, but nothing more than that.

This technique is often used in working with trauma. For example, if a girl feels guilty about being molested by her father, an outside observer may note that it was the father who molested the daughter and it was not her fault.

Trauma Diary. Another technique used for working with traumas is the ABC Diary for Trauma. This is, in fact, the same ABC diary, but here significant life events are recorded, and the conclusions that the individual has drawn from them, and then rational responses to these conclusions are written down.

The "Stop!" technique. The "Stop!" technique is also used to work with maladaptive thoughts, when the client, when such thoughts arise, should loudly say to them: "Stop!" and they should disappear. (This is probably the most ineffective technique of CBT, but despite its claimed scientific, for some reason, it continues to be taught).

Systematic sensitization and exposure. We will unite sensitization and exposure into one group of techniques, as we have already talked about them quite a lot. The essence comes down to the fact that the person met with the frightening object and lived through the emotions connected with it, so that they, according to the law of the verbal reflex, came to extinction.

Setting Limits. Another set of techniques I have grouped and called setting limits. This includes anything that involves limiting behavior and its exposure. For example, this is how to limit the number of calories eaten per week; the number of times a client seeks help to compensate for their loneliness; and the amount of time it takes for an OCD patient to start performing their rituals.

To summarize, cognitive-behavioral psychotherapy is based on an understanding of the origin of various human reactions, negative emotions, negative experiences, and unconstructive behavior. This therapy considers human reactions as a result of triggering instantaneous, sometimes unconsidered automatic stereotypical attitudes, some learned beliefs, and painful attitudes.

All these cognitions are subconscious and therefore it takes time and persistence to deal with them, let alone change them to positive life-affirming ones. The cognitive-behavioral approach shows the client that nothing is impossible and forms further behavior that will allow them to get out of the deadlock, begin to develop as a person, enjoy life, control their fears, and no longer "be a prisoner of them".

In conclusion, Aaron Beck himself helped people until the last day of his life and died at the age of 100. At the same time, all this time he kept an ABC diary and challenged his thoughts. His therapy is by far the most popular and most researched to date.

CHAPTER 1
UNDERSTANDING YOUR STATE OF MIND

"You can run away, run very fast and far away, but you can't run away from yourself."

- Cecelia Ahern, Irish writer.

In this opening chapter, we dive into some reflective exercises to get a handle on our emotions and overall well-being. It's all about the stage for personal growth and emotional healing.

The next exercise is a simple way for you to check in with your emotions so you can get a better handle on how you're feeling. It's all about helping you understand yourself a bit better right from the start.

So, let's start! First up, we're going to go over some exercises that are designed to help you gain a clear and honest look at how you're feeling right now and what's going on with overall wellness.

Identifying feelings

Let's kick things off with the three-step emotional check-in. It's a straightforward but powerful process that's all about helping you recognize and tune into how you're feeling right now in a mindful and structured way.

Step 1: Pause and Focus

1.1 Find a quiet space where you won't be disturbed for a few minutes.
1.2 Sit comfortably and close your eyes. Take a few deep breaths to center yourself.

Step 2: Identify Your Emotions

2.1 It could be difficult, especially the first time and I must admit that we mostly feel a few emotions at the same time. So, it is ok if you have several feelings, just try to identify them.

Ask yourself, "What am I feeling right now?". Allow whatever emotions are present to surface. It might be one evident emotion or a mix of several feelings.

Step 3: Acknowledge and Record

3.1 Once you have identified your emotions, open your eyes and write them down in a journal or notebook.

3.2 Briefly note any events or thoughts that might have triggered these emotions.

3.3 Rating your well-being. We'll check in on how you're feeling with the emotions tracker. It will help you keep tabs on your emotional state over time.

Below is the tracking system for you to use whenever you want, for as long as you want. I suggest rating how you're doing three times a day for at least a week #1. In the future doing this regularly will help you spot any trends or shifts in how you're feeling.

It is recommended to use pens or pencils of different colors. This way it will be more clearly visible. Use red color to fill in the fields of negative emotions and any other color to fill in the fields of positive emotions.

Let me show you how to use this table in my example:

| | Time | Event/Thoughts | Emotions | |
			Positive	Negative
Day #1	Morning	Woke up this morning	morning glory	feeling of fatigue anxiety irritability
		Looked at myself in the mirror and saw my swollen face		disappointment despair sense of injustice
	Afternoon	Talking on the phone with mom	pleasure to hear	boredom irritation
	Evening	Ate some chocolate	enjoyment	sense of guilt

You should practice this check-in several times a day, especially during moments of transition, like before a meal or at the end of a work session.

Over time, you may notice patterns in your emotional responses, which can provide valuable insights into your emotional health triggers.

	Time	Event/Thoughts	Emotions	
			Positive	Negative
Day #1	Morning			
	Afternoon			
	Evening			
Day #2	Morning			
	Afternoon			
	Evening			
Day #3	Morning			
	Afternoon			
	Evening			
Day #4	Morning			
	Afternoon			

	Evening			
Day #5	**Morning**			
	Afternoon			
	Evening			
Day #6	**Morning**			
	Afternoon			
	Evening			
Day #7	**Morning**			
	Afternoon			
	Evening			

Once you've got some data, I've got some questions to help you think about your weekly scores. After completing a week with the tracker, taking a moment to reflect on your experiences can give you some real insight into your emotional state. Here are some questions to help you out:

1. Looking back at your week, what general trends do you notice in your well-being scores? Were there more highs and lows, or was it a mix?

_____

_____

_____

2. Can you identify specific days or times when your well-being scores were particularly high or low? What do you think contributed to these fluctuations?

_____

_____

_____

3. Were there any events or interactions this week that significantly impacted your emotional outlook? How did these moments affect your well-being scores?

_____

_____

_____

4. Reflect on how you managed your emotions throughout the week. Which coping strategies did you find most helpful?

_____

_____

_____

5. Did anything surprise you about your well-being scores this week? What new insights have you gained about your emotional well-being?

_____

_____

_____

6. Based on your tracker, what areas of your emotional well-being need more attention or improvement?

_____

_____

_____

7. Considering your reflections, what goals would you like to set for your emotional well-being for the upcoming week?

_____

_____

_____

8. How did your self-care practices influence your well-being scores? What self-care activities could you integrate into your routine?

_____

_____

_____

Thinking through these questions can help you understand how your emotions have been playing out over the past week. It's all about guiding you toward a more mindful and proactive way of taking care of your emotional well-being.

Diving into the world of emotions

When it's gray outside the window and the morning coffee stains your shirt, a bad mood is assured. But good news can turn all problems into nothing. It seems that emotions do control us.

Emergency - those are the words experts at the American Pediatric Association use to describe the current emotional health of U.S. children and adolescents.

The coronavirus has shaken the stability and mental health of not only children, but many adults around the world, and even after the pandemic, emotional tensions have hardly diminished.

If external conditions have such a strong impact on internal emotional well-being, is there anything we can do to fix it? Or at least minimize the negative impact of bad news to help people feel better? It is possible. But first, we need to understand exactly how we feel.

It happens that we live for years and do not even know what those or other feelings that we experience can be called. We just live, good or bad, it does not matter, not many in childhood were taught to determine their emotions. And there was no such subject in the school program. If you have difficulties in doing the exercise above, do not be sad, it is quite normal. This exercise is aimed at diving deeper into your emotional world and understanding your states. After all, it is through emotions that we understand our state. Emotions are our guides and navigators. Having understood what you feel, and this is a huge step, we will go further and find the answer to the question "Why?". This is the reason why a psychologist will relentlessly ask you about your feelings and such a sentence as "and how you felt at that" is very popular in working on yourself, even if it is not usual.

Types of emotions

Human emotions play a crucial role, from influencing our communication with the outside world to our physical health and the quality of our decision-making.

By breaking down the basic types of emotions, we can better identify them and more easily relate them to a particular palette of our feelings.

Attention - we are entering a zone of scientific turbulence. The fact is that scientists still cannot agree on the exact definition of the types and number of emotions. For example, in the XVII century Rene Descartes allocated six basic emotions from which all other emotions grow. They were **joy, sadness, surprise, desire, love, and hate.**

In the 70s of the twentieth century, psychologist Paul Ekman named the same number but collected a different set of feelings. According to his definition, **happiness, sadness, disgust, fear, surprise, and anger** should be included among those inherent in all people and cultures. He later expanded and added **pride, shame, embarrassment, and excitement to** his list.

In 2014, a group of scientists from Glasgow proposed a serious reduction in the number of basic emotions. In a study, they asked subjects to identify the emotions of animated faces created and found that anger and disgust were perceived to be similar. Just like fear and surprise.

For example, anger and disgust share the same wrinkled nose, and surprise and fear share the same raised eyebrows. Thus, the scientists concluded that these emotions are the product of an evolving society. And they left joy, sadness, fear/surprise and anger/disgust as "basic" emotions.

We can think of basic emotions as roots around which branches of many other emotions grow. Modern researchers have identified at least 27 different categories of emotions and their gradients.

Here's an extensive but not comprehensive list:

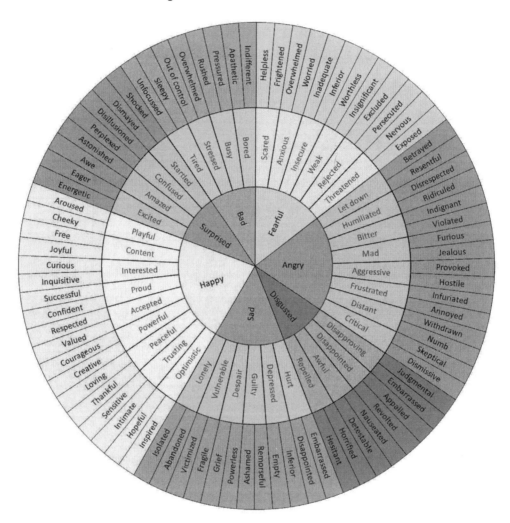

Where emotions "grow" from

Knowing basic emotions allows us to better understand how we feel. But can we say that they will be the same for all people?

In the past, scientists have agreed on the understanding of emotions as innate, biologically determined reactions to certain challenges and opportunities. It was believed that their architect was evolution itself, whose primary function was the survival of the species.

Regardless of culture or environment, people experience fear in the face of danger.

Fear is important because it helped ancestors to escape from danger in time. Or parents: no matter what kind of society they live in, but looking at their children, most of them will feel a sense of love.

Researcher Lisa Feldman-Barrett refutes the classic theory in her book ""How Emotions Are Born".

Summarizing a grand array of data, she came up with the idea that emotions have no innate nature. These reactions are not automatic but developed in response to experience and prior knowledge.

The researcher denies the universality of human emotions by showing a portrait of tennis player Serena Williams. Some observers saw in her face a state of agony, although in fact, it was a triumph after a winning match.

We can easily get confused in interpreting the expression of emotions. And that proves their individuality.

On this basis, Feldman-Barrett comes to the definition of emotions as social knowledge. It is like muffins and cupcakes - the essence may be the same, but different families will call the dish different names.

How emotions affect us

Emotions do not exist apart from us, just as we and our cmotions do not exist apart from society.

Therefore, much experiences-including empathy, shame, guilt, friendship, love, gratitude, anger, revenge, and gossip are simultaneously mechanisms for cooperation in a group.

There is even a view of emotion not as an isolated phenomenon, but as a language of communication. In this way, we gradually come to the idea that our emotional state determines the achievements and successes of each individual.

When we feel bad, it's harder to exercise, work, plan, or even just take the right medication on time. And the longer we stay in this state of decline, the harder it is to get out of it.

Emotions also directly influence our decisions. Anger, fear, or sadness compel some actions, while gratitude or pride compel others.

Research shows that through behavioral modifications, you can **reduce the risk of many diseases that** significantly impact quality of life, including heart disease, diabetes, and cancer.

Evidence suggests that emotions can improve the quality of health decisions.

Taking care of your emotional state has physical results. Stress, anxiety, and other emotions that are commonly described by the words "bad mood" lead to a deterioration of the immune system.

The stress hormone cortisol can suppress the effectiveness of the immune system.

Stress can also have an indirect effect on the immune system, as a person may choose unhealthy behavioral strategies to "improve" their condition: they start abusing alcohol or smoking.

Stimulation of the vagus nerve (nervus vagus) can improve your emotional state. It is the nerve that determines how quickly a person can cope with and recover from stressful situations.

By the way, the vagus nerve is also responsible for the "butterflies in the stomach" that accompany our crushes.

An increase in the number of positive emotions increases the tone of the vagus nerve. The effect extends to the perception of social connections. This is why it is easier to achieve results when we are in a good mood.

How to get your emotions under control

It seems that since negative emotions are so harmful, you should just suppress them.

It turns out that this is a bad idea. Refusal to express and manifest one's feelings is harmful to both physical and emotional health. And leads, among other things, to depression. Therefore, bad emotions should be lived.

One of the best ways to live through emotions, rather than drive them into yourself, is to name them.

It can take time to learn to discern the full emotional palette. The basic underlying feelings can become the roots from which the lush branches of your emotional scale will grow.

This acceptance will help you learn to live with any emotion and not suffer from things going wrong.

Psychologists recommend that you write down all your feelings for at least one week, checking them every few hours. This exercise will help you learn how to feel and build up your emotional vocabulary.

Visualizing the future

"Whatever the mind can conceive and believe, it can accomplish."

- Napoleon Hill, a worldwide American self-help author.

What comes to mind when you think of visualization exercises? What if I told you that I discovered something profound about visualization? Why Visualization is Not Just "Seeing Pictures" in your mind. I've discovered a simple process that suggests that everything you thought you knew about "seeing pictures in your mind" is wrong. Especially when it comes to memorization techniques, memory palace, and all things related to mnemonics.

There are at least 8 modes: kinesthetic, auditory, visual, emotional, conceptual, olfactory, gustatory, and spatial. And "seeing" is only one of them!

Multiple modes of visualization don't mean you don't have to 'see' mentally." Now that you know there are so many different ways to visualize, could you try a few alternative visualization methods?

If you said yes, or at least nodded your head in the affirmative, that's great. Read on.

Did you know that visualization is much more than meditation, and can serve you in your daily life as a mature student in practice? Again, it's more than seeing pictures in your mind. The ability to conjure up mental images in your mind is a great skill. Visualization is most effective when it is embedded in a multi-sensory experience.

How to develop the power of visualization

Everything begins with a thought. Every action and every word is first created in the human imagination. The ability to see things before we realize them is what allows us to follow and achieve our dreams. Simply put, the more clearly, we visualize the future we want, the greater the chances of that future coming to pass.

The brain sees no difference between real and imagined action. Some studies confirm that when a person thinks about an action (even if the body is at complete rest), it activates nerve pathways in the brain as if it were happening.

Many successful people benefit from the power of visualization. Olympic champions, for example, visualize in detail the feelings they have when they receive a medal.

The power of visualization can be developed. Here are five steps you need to climb to become a professional in this area. Tip: do not do the second exercise until you have had tangible success with the first.

The first exercise

Find a picture and take some time to analyze it. Memorize as many details as you can. Then close your eyes and try to reconstruct it from memory. Any details: color, shapes, feelings, meaning, freckles on your face. Open your eyes and compare it to the photograph. Practice this exercise until you can completely reconstruct the picture. By the way, this technique is called the Aivazovsky method.

The second exercise

Switch to three-dimensional mode. Take some small objects. For example, a pen or your keys. Analyze all the details and remember them. Take your time.

Now close your eyes and visualize this object in detail. Turn it around in your imagination, look at it from different angles. Put this object on an imaginary table, drop it on the floor, and imagine how it will behave. Taste it. Of course, all of this should happen only in your imagination.

The third exercise

This exercise is in addition to the first one. This time, look at a real object and then remove it from your field of vision, but keep your eyes open. With your eyes open, visualize the object. Visualize it as clearly as if you could see it. Do the same as in the previous exercise - throw it on the ground, and put it on the table.

Fourth exercise

When you get to the fourth step, you deserve to have a little fun. Place yourself mentally in a place you like. It doesn't matter if you've ever been there. It could be a castle, an art gallery, a beach, or even a scene from a movie. Don't think about the location, be there, feel the touches, smell the smells, hear the sounds. First one by one, and then all together. Is it cold or warm? Is there a breeze or a draft? Talk to someone in your scene.

Exercise five

Total immersion. You are in an imaginary location. Interact with all the things that are there. Take a rock in your hand, and sit on a bench. Have someone play music there. Live in that location for about 10 minutes. You don't need to imagine something quite incredible and impossible, let the laws of physics exist. How do you feel?

Detail and Realism. Realism is the most essential thing in visualization and thus compares favorably to mere daydreaming. Everything you visualize must be so real that you believe it. Engage all your senses.

From any fantasy, you end up getting nothing because reality is completely different. Visualization, on the other hand, goes much further. Your brain begins to think that what you visualize happened. If you visualize yourself in some castle you saw in a picture and your heart doesn't start beating excitedly, you're just fantasizing. The amount of detail starts to create realism and you believe it is happening.

So, let's apply the power of visualization to your goals.

Focus on the positive. We often focus on negative things, so change that approach.

Possess it, not desire it. If you want something, imagine that it already exists in your life and behave accordingly.

Be persistent. It's not easy to do this every day for a long period. Visualization works, which means there is value in persistence and habit formation.

Be specific. Many people have vague goals, so they don't get much accomplished. Present specific amounts, specific items, specific people, and places.

Visualization has tremendous power that anyone can develop. Practice it daily. In any case, the exercises in this chapter of the book will at least allow you to develop your creative imagination and, even better, enhance your cognitive skills, which will inherently make you a much stronger and more developed person.

Exercise "My delightful life in 1 year."

I have tried several times to tell you more about this method, which I use regularly and which works for me, but I kept putting it off. I feel like I'm not being completely honest in this story yet, and I think I've figured out why. The thing is, the goal-setting process alone is not enough. You need to grow two additional tentacles before you can talk about it boldly.

The first is to put together from disparate goals a unified picture of where you want to get to.

The second is to clothe goals with tools that help achieve them. Today is about a painting. The setting is as follows. Periodically, I write down 100 goals I want to accomplish in a year. I spend two or three days doing this. I don't usually do this from scratch, most of the material is from the previous year. Then I work diligently on them, complete 60-70, carry over the unfulfilled ones, and repeat the process. 65% may seem like a good performance, but why am I not doing the rest? My current thinking is that they lose relevance and get boring. The further away from the beginning of the year, the harder it is to remember exactly what I put into each goal.

A list of goals is useful, but it's not enough. It is abstract and doesn't add up to a coherent picture in your head. This isn't a problem on the horizon of a day or week. You write down the tasks, take the first one, and do it. But as soon as you need to plan for the long term, problems of priority, focus, and consistency come out. Without a clear picture of the outcome, you run the risk of getting bogged down in a constant stream of urgent tasks. You have to learn to manage this process if you want to get to a certain point in the future.

As social animals, we are intrinsically tied to storytelling. Our entire culture is built on them. From the dirty joke of a contagious coworker at the water cooler to the latest high-tech viar games. A story is a great addition to the goal-setting process, too. You can use it to tie individual items into a cohesive picture and throw in a sensory experience. A sensory experience will breathe life into a flat list and keep you motivated during tough times. I've found the right exercise.

The exercise is called "My Delightful Life in 1 Year" and helps you create a vision for your life in the future. It was invented by Milton Glaser and started to be used in his work with students. He is the designer who came up with the I ♥ NY logo that resonated with millions of people.

The point of the exercise is very simple. You need to write an essay about how you see your ideal life in some time. I find it convenient to take one year at a time, but you can set goals for a year, five or more.

Describe all the areas of your life that matter to you. Try to work out as many details as possible. Here are examples of questions to answer:

1. How are you doing with your health? How do you feel every day?

_____

_____

2. How, where and how often do you train?

_____

_____

3. What do you eat, do you follow any special diets?

_____

_____

4. What is your relationship with alcohol and other addictive substances?

_____

_____

5. Are you sleeping well? Do you engage in meditation and other mindfulness practices?

_____

_____

6. What is your relationship with your family and friends? Where and with whom do you live? How do you spend time with your loved ones?

_____

_____

7. Where do you live? What does your apartment or house look like? What kind of repairs and furniture does it have? Where do the windows face?

_____

_____

8. Do you have a car? What kind? Where do you drive it? How do you take care of it?

_____

_____

9. What is your money situation? How much have you saved? What do you think about investing?

_____

_____

10. Where do you work, employed or self-employed? What kind of company is it? What position are you in? How long have you been there? Where do you aspire to go?

_____

_____

11. How and what are you learning? What skills do you want to develop? What books are you reading?

_____

_____

12. What is your big dream? What do you want out of life?

13. Have you found a way to share what you have in abundance with the world?

_____

_____

14. In the last block, add a detailed description of a day in your life. Where and how did you wake up? What did you have for breakfast? Where were you and what did you do during the day?

_____

_____

If some areas do not resonate with your current state, cross them out. If something important is missing, write it down. Sit down in a comfortable place where no one will distract you for a few hours and let your stream of consciousness flow onto paper. Try not to edit in the process. Write by hand. There's some forgotten magic to it and it's easier to fall into a flow state. Set ambitious goals and describe a truly ideal life, even if it's unclear now how you'll get there.

When you finish your essay, save it in a convenient place where you can reread it regularly. For example, I wrote it in a paper notebook and transferred it to a notebook on a shared drive so I could access it from any device. It's worth re-reading the essay at least once a year afterward as part of the goal-setting process. Write out from the picture of the future the most important points that need to be worked on first. Then add to your usual framework of working with goals. We tend to overestimate what we can accomplish in a year and underestimate what we can accomplish in five to ten years. In ten years of focused, continuous work, you may well achieve the ideal picture you've painted for yourself. This is a working methodology from the realm of the rational.

Practitioners of this exercise also claim that the effects show up in the realm of the irrational as well. A clear picture of the future, written once, will keep you on track and help you make decisions in difficult times. It will work on its own, without active participation on your part. Such is the power of visualization. Once spoken aloud, it tends to come true.

One last argument in favor. When the future finally arrives, it will be interesting to compare whether or not that's where you ended up going. This will be difficult to do if no direction is set initially.

I spent four hours on the exercise in two sessions. I feel slightly drained, positive, and increasingly confident about the future. I wrote it myself. I invite you to do this exercise with me.

A letter to you in the future

"Use the current time in such a way that in old age you will not blame yourself for youth lived in vain."

- Giovanni Boccaccio, an Italian writer, poet and humanist

A letter to the future is an intimate message addressed to yourself, which you will open and read after a certain period (in this case, a year). It is an opportunity to immerse yourself and share your thoughts, feelings, and plans for the future with yourself. After all, who better to know yourself than you?

Write a letter to your inner child - yourself. Open up, be sincere. Tell about what inspires you, makes you happy, or worries you. Think about your current state of happiness, work, dreams, and desires for the future.

Below are questions to help you better understand yourself and your goals.

1. What inspires me?
2. Am I happy now?
3. Do I love my job?
4. What do I want to change in my life?
5. What brings me the most joy?
6. What are my dreams?
7. How did I see myself in the past and how do I see myself in the future?
8. What do I usually do in my free time, and do I want to keep doing it?

9. Where do I live now and where do I dream of living in the future?
10. Where have I traveled to and what did I like best?

Put the letter you have written in an envelope and seal it. Don't forget to sign the envelope and write the date when you can open it. Hide the letter in a private place where no one, including you, can accidentally stumble upon it. Also, set a reminder on your phone's calendar so you don't forget to open the envelope a year from now.

Chapter 2

CHECK YOUR ANXIETY LEVEL

"Fear is not in danger at all, it is in ourselves."

\- Stendhal, a French writer

Definition of anxiety

What is anxiety?

Anxiety is an emotional discomfort that is associated with the expectation and anticipation of unpleasant experiences or dangers. Even if everything around is good and prosperous, a person experiences a background feeling of impending trouble.

Anxiety in psychology can mean a short-term emotional state, or it can be a stable character trait of a person. Anxiety as an emotion is peculiar to all people and is necessary for the optimal adaptation of a person to the surrounding world. Anxiety, as a part of a person's personality, is a violation of his personal development and interferes with a full-fledged life in society.

A constant feeling of anxiety and fear is a consequence of intrapersonal conflict. It can be a contradiction between the image of the ideal self and the real self, which is a discrepancy between the level of self-esteem and the level of a person's claims. Anxiety always signals the need to satisfy a need, and the feeling of constant anxiety is an indicator that the need is not satisfied.

The feeling of anxiety is also a fact of the dissatisfaction with the social-psychological needs of a person.

Increased anxiety is closely related to the patterns between the emotional and motivational needs spheres of personality. Intrapersonal conflict leads to unsatisfied needs, which creates tension and a state of anxiety.

Once persistent fear and anxiety become entrenched in a person's psyche, this new part of the personality can negatively influence further motivations for behavior - their communications with others, motivation to succeed, life activities, and actions.

Anxiety, along with emotions such as fear and hope, is in a special position. As Fritz Perls, the great German psychiatrist, said, "The formula for anxiety is very simple. Anxiety is a gap, between now and then".

Symptoms of anxiety

Psychologically, anxiety manifests itself as preoccupation, tension, nervousness, and worry. It is characterized by such feelings as helplessness, uncertainty, insecurity, impending failure, loneliness, and inability to make a decision.

Physically, anxiety manifests itself in rapid heartbeat and breathing, increased blood pressure, decreased sensitivity, and increased arousal. Stimuli that were neutral before the onset of anxiety become negatively colored.

The person begins to have sleep disorders - he/she cannot fall asleep for a long time, sleeps restlessly, and may wake up very early and never sleep again. Or, on the contrary, they cannot wake up on time, wake up late and feel broken.

Appetite disorders also occur. Either an excessive increase in appetite, when a person eats his anxiety, and even if he eats his favorite dish in a comfortable environment, he does not feel a sense of satiation and satisfaction with what he has eaten, as a result of which he eats more than necessary. Or, on the contrary, the person experiences a painful lack of appetite. Every day he begins to skip some meals more and more and eats much less than he should, and he does not notice it himself. Anxiety is more often a consequence of excessive eating and depressive anxiety - lack of appetite.

In addition, the emergence of anxiety is accompanied by a change in attitude towards alcohol. As a rule, it manifests itself as an obsessive thought in the evening on the way home: "Why don't I have a drink?". There seems to be no reason, but the inner feeling of a bad mood pushes me to drink and relieve stress. It becomes an attribute of daily lifestyle - a bottle of beer, or a glass of cognac in the evenings. In the kitchen cupboard, there is a constant bottle of alcohol and every meal is accompanied by a small amount of alcohol. All would be nothing, but alcohol does not solve psychological problems, moreover, alcohol dependence begins to develop, and the main cause of anxiety remains unresolved.

Causes of Anxiety

Feeling anxious without a reason is evidence of the presence of negative emotional experiences in a person. Anxious people have a significant predominance of orientation to external criteria. In addition, anxious people often feel the need for increased self-control, even in minor aspects of the situation. Failure to do so provokes even greater levels of anxiety and the emergence of new negative experiences.

An important role in negative emotional experience plays not so much the fact of its experience, but rather its firm memorization and reproduction in memory.

Peculiarities of family upbringing

Family upbringing also has a great influence on the development of anxiety. It is impossible to speak about any specific disorder, as their range is quite wide: hyper-parenting over the child, increased expectations, high demands, and poor relationships between parents and family members.

Emotional problems are more common in people who were raised by parents who were prone to nervousness, irritability, and depression. Parents of anxious children are more likely to experience worries and fears, while calm children are raised by balanced and positive adults.

When an adult experiences a sense of instability and perceives a constant threat, this is instantly transmitted to the child. This is often expressed in excessive concern and fear for the child's life and health. This causes the child to feel insecure and defenseless, which persists and is reinforced over the years.

Post-traumatic stress

Post-traumatic stress disorder can be identified as an external cause of anxiety. Post-traumatic stress disorder is a severe emotional experience, such as feelings of helplessness, terror, and intense fear, which arise as a result of a single incident, or as a result of repeated traumas and a long stay in a stressful situation. The consequence of such experiences in adults is increased anxiety.

This applies to people who have survived an accident, been involved in war, an environmental disaster, or gross violence.

Intrapersonal sources of anxiety.

An important source of anxiety can be identified as a person's internal conflict, which is directly related to his self-esteem and attitude toward himself. It is not characteristic of anxious people to change, adapt to difficulties, and correct their shortcomings, which distinguishes emotionally well-off people. On the contrary, anxious people are characterized by a fixation on the past or on a very distant future, on the period on which they are unable to influence.

The reasons that cause anxiety are manifold. They are also divided into subjective and objective causes. The subjective reasons include those related to the nervous perception of the outcome of the upcoming event. Objective causes include extreme conditions associated with the uncertainty of the outcome of the situation: fatigue, mental disturbance, and anxiety about one's health.

Constant worrying about your life and worrying about your loved ones is a state of mental tension or anxiety. Almost every second person suffers from this ailment. The consequences of frequent manifestation of anxiety, as a rule, are disappointing. The state of constant anxiety leads to difficulties in the nervous system and can be the cause of nervousness, headaches, depression, and panic attacks. The feeling of anxiety itself is exhausting. It can be felt through chills throughout the body, a feeling of a "lump in the throat". Experiencing constant anxiety, a person often feels fatigue and a lack of moral and physical strength. This is because all the energy is spent on suppressing anxiety and its displacement.

It can be very difficult to get rid of the complications of constant anxiety. Therefore, if you feel prolonged and unreasonable anxiety, you need to think about how to get rid of it.

Summarizing, it can be noted that anxiety in the soul without reason is a stable personal formation, which was formed at different age stages. In junior school and preschool age, the beginning of anxiety was provoked by the situation in the family and relationships with parents. It was then that such qualities as vulnerability, tendency to resentment, and aggravated reaction to the attitude of others began to take shape in the child. This, as well as a predisposition to remember negative rather than positive events, leads to the accumulation of negative experiences, which is subsequently expressed in the consolidation of anxiety as a personal character trait.

In adolescence, feelings of anxiety are anchored based on internal conflict with oneself, the contradiction between the "I-ideal" and the "I-real".

The causes of anxiety are in one way or another related to the unmet needs specific to each age period.

Types of Anxiety.

Anxiety is a psychological trait, a person's tendency to experience a state of anxiety. Most often anxiety is related to the expectation of social consequences of his failure or success. Anxiety is closely related to stress.

Modern science shows great interest in the problem of anxiety. This interest is shown in many scientific studies, where this problem occupies a significant position and is analyzed in a psychological aspect.

It is generally believed that the problem of anxiety as a psychological problem was first subjected to special consideration in the works of Sigmund Freud. He noted that anxiety is a reaction to danger, unknown and undefined.

There are several types of anxiety in psychology, but the most common are:

Social anxiety is when a person feels uncomfortable being among large crowds of people.

Public Anxiety - this feeling of anxiety is acute at any public event.

Post-traumatic anxiety is a state of persistent anxiety that appears after experiencing psychological trauma.

Existential anxiety is a person's awareness of the fact that they may die someday.

A divided anxiety state is when a person experiences a severe anxiety attack if they find themselves away from a place or a particular person.

On the one hand, anxiety is the experience of anxiety itself, in which a person feels uncomfortable, and therefore seeks to get rid of this feeling as soon as possible. On the other hand, anxiety signals real and possible "malfunctions".

Diagnosing an Anxiety Condition.

The most informative and in my opinion requiring minimal effort test to identify the level of anxiety is the Spielberger-Hanin test.

The Spielberger-Hanin test belongs to the number of methods that investigate the psychological phenomenon of anxiety. The Spielberger-Hanin diagnostic is the only methodology that allows differentiated measurement of anxiety as a personality trait and as a state related to the current situation. This test will help to determine the severity of anxiety in the personality structure.

Personality anxiety characterizes a stable tendency to perceive a wide range of situations as threatening, to react to such situations with a state of anxiety. Reactive anxiety is characterized by tension, restlessness, and nervousness. Very high reactive anxiety causes a violation of attention, sometimes a violation of fine coordination. Very high personality anxiety directly correlates with the presence of neurotic conflict, with emotional and neurotic breakdowns and psychosomatic diseases.

Measurement of anxiety as a property of personality is especially important because this property largely determines the behavior of the subject. A certain level of anxiety is a natural and obligatory feature of an active personality. Each person has his own optimal, or desirable, level of anxiety - this is the so-called useful anxiety. A person's assessment of his state in this respect is an essential component of self-control and self-education.

The Spielberger test consists of 20 statements relating to anxiety as a state (state anxiety, reactive or situational anxiety) and 20 statements to determine anxiety as a disposition, a personality trait (trait anxiety).

Instruction

Read each of the following sentences carefully and cross out the number in the appropriate box on the right, depending on how you feel at the moment. Do not think about the questions for long, as there are no right or wrong answers.

The Spielberger-Hanin test is administered using two forms:

Form No. 1 for measuring indicators of situational (reactive) anxiety:

	Judgment	No, it's not	I guess so	That's right	Quite right
1	I'm calm.	1	2	3	4
2	I'm in no danger	1	2	3	4
3	I'm under a lot of pressure	1	2	3	4
4	I'm inhibited	1	2	3	4
5	I feel free	1	2	3	4
6	I'm upset.	1	2	3	4
7	I'm worried about possible failure	1	2	3	4
8	I feel a sense of peace of mind	1	2	3	4
9	I'm alarmed	1	2	3	4
10	I feel a sense of inner satisfaction	1	2	3	4
11	I'm confident	1	2	3	4
12	I'm nervous	1	2	3	4
13	I can't find a place	1	2	3	4
14	I'm strung out.	1	2	3	4
15	I feel no stiffness, no tension	1	2	3	4
16	I'm satisfied	1	2	3	4
17	I'm concerned	1	2	3	4
18	I'm too horny and I'm not comfortable	1	2	3	4
19	I'm happy	1	2	3	4
20	It's my pleasure.	1	2	3	4

Instructions for the Personality Anxiety Test: Read each of the following sentences carefully. Cross out the number in the appropriate box on the right, depending on how you usually feel. Do not think about the questions for long, as there are no right or wrong answers.

Form No. 2 for measuring the level of personality anxiety.

	Judgment	Never	Rarely	Often	Always
1	I can be in an uplifting mood	1	2	3	4
2	I can be irritable	1	2	3	4
3	I can easily get frustrated	1	2	3	4
4	I wish I could be as fortunate as the others	1	2	3	4
5	I go through a lot of trouble and can't forget about it for a long time	1	2	3	4
6	I feel energized and eager to work	1	2	3	4
7	I'm calm, cool, and collected.	1	2	3	4
8	I'm worried about the possible difficulties	1	2	3	4
9	I worry too much about nothing	1	2	3	4
10	I can be quite happy	1	2	3	4
11	I take everything personally	1	2	3	4
12	I lack self-confidence	1	2	3	4
13	I feel defenseless	1	2	3	4
14	I try to avoid critical situations	1	2	3	4
15	I get mopey	1	2	3	4
16	I can be satisfied	1	2	3	4
17	Stuff distracts me and worries me.	1	2	3	4
18	There are times when I feel like a failure.	1	2	3	4
19	I'm a balanced person	1	2	3	4
20	I get anxious when I think about my business and worries	1	2	3	4

EDUCATION

Scores for each of the scales are awarded according to the key. Key to the methodology:

Table 1 (Situational)	Situational Anxiety Scale	Table 2 (Personal)	Personality Anxiety Scale
Judgment number	Points for answers	Judgment number	Points for answers
1	4 3 2 1	1	4 3 2 1
2	4 3 2 1	2	1 2 3 4
3	1 2 3 4	3	4 3 2 1
4	1 2 3 4	4	1 2 3 4
5	4 3 2 1	5	1 2 3 4
6	1 2 3 4	6	4 3 2 1
7	1 2 3 4	7	4 3 2 1
8	4 3 2 1	8	1 2 3 4
9	1 2 3 4	9	1 2 3 4
10	4 3 2 1	10	4 3 2 1
11	4 3 2 1	11	1 2 3 4
12	1 2 3 4	12	1 2 3 4
13	1 2 3 4	13	1 2 3 4
14	1 2 3 4	14	1 2 3 4
15	4 3 2 1	15	1 2 3 4
16	4 3 2 1	16	4 3 2 1
17	1 2 3 4	17	1 2 3 4
18	1 2 3 4	18	1 2 3 4
19	4 3 2 1	19	4 3 2 1
20	4 3 2 1	20	1 2 3 4

The total number of points for each of the scales is calculated, and the indicators are compared with the normative ones:

up to **30 points** - low anxiety.

31 to 44 points - moderate anxiety.

45 and over - pronounced anxiety.

When analyzing the results of self-assessment, it should be borne in mind that the total final score for each subscale can range from 20 to 80 points. The higher the total score, the higher the level of anxiety (situational or personal).

Individuals categorized as highly anxious tend to perceive a threat to their self-esteem and life activity in a wide range of situations and react with a very pronounced state of anxiety. If a psychological test expresses a high index of personality anxiety in a subject, it gives reason to assume that he or she has a state of anxiety in a variety of situations, especially when they relate to the assessment of his or her competence and prestige.

Individuals with high anxiety should be encouraged to develop a sense of confidence and success. They need to shift the emphasis from external demanding, categorical, high importance in setting tasks to meaningful reflection of activities and specific planning of subtasks.

For low-anxious people, on the contrary, it is required to awaken activity, emphasize motivational components of activity, arouse interest, and highlight the sense of responsibility in solving certain tasks.

The state of reactive (situational) anxiety occurs when getting into a stressful situation and is characterized by subjective discomfort, tension, anxiety, and vegetative excitement. Naturally, this state is characterized by instability in time and different intensities depending on the strength of the impact of the stressful situation. Thus, the value of the final indicator on this subscale allows us to assess not only the level of actual anxiety of the test subject but also to determine whether he/she is under the influence of a stressful situation and what is the intensity of this impact on him/her.

Personality anxiety is a constitutional trait that causes a tendency to perceive threats in a wide range of situations. With high personality anxiety, each of these situations will have a stressful effect on the subject and cause him or her significant anxiety. Very high personality anxiety directly correlates with the presence of neurotic conflict, with emotional and neurotic breakdowns and psychosomatic diseases.

Comparison of the results for both subscales makes it possible to assess the individual significance of the stressful situation for the subject. Due to its relative simplicity and efficiency, the Spielberger scale is widely used in the clinic for various purposes: to determine the severity of anxiety, to assess the state in dynamics, etc. The Spielberger scale is used in the clinic.

Anxiety as a personality trait means a motive or acquired behavioral disposition that obliges an individual to perceive a wide range of objectively safe circumstances as containing a threat, prompting the individual to react to them with states of anxiety, the intensity of which does not correspond to the magnitude of the real danger. The Spielberger Reactive and Personality Anxiety Scale is the only methodology that allows differentiated measurement of anxiety as a personality trait and as a state.

12 simple ways to calm down and not get stressed out

Sometimes we look for complicated recipes to improve the quality of life. We think: "If I go to yoga, I will be calmer immediately. And of course, we don't go to yoga. And we have the most heartfelt excuse as to why we feel so bad. There's no good yoga in the neighborhood! Sad.

Nevertheless, there are primitive, quick self-help techniques that can be used when anxiety levels are elevated. These techniques are widely known and used in cognitive-behavioral therapy.

Method 1. Distract yourself from something.

This way to relieve emotional tension is suitable in those cases when you are trapped, cornered, and can not escape anywhere. For example, you are sitting at a meeting and listening to your boss, inwardly boiling. You can't escape, but distracting yourself by contemplating something extraneous, neutral, and engrossing yourself in this extraneous is the best way to avoid getting yourself worked up over nothing.

For example: "What a manicure Masha has, though.... I wonder how she did it?"

It only works if you understand the benefit of such a strategy - don't look at nastiness, don't listen to nastiness. If you like to boil over and get into arguments, that's your right.

Method 2. Leave the irritating situation.

Did something sadden you at someone else's birthday party? At a picnic? You can't stand some group, public, social networking page? Do you dream of removing an unpleasant person from your friends list?

Okay, quickly out of the group for good. Banned the argumentative provocateur, the troll, the boor, the fool. Deleted your profile, if anything.

Quickly called a cab (don't be stingy) kissed the hostess and rushed home - away from the party, away from kebabs, away from the irritating, emotionally charged zone.

Method 3. Drink some water.

Now that's the crown recipe of all the brilliant GPs who don't peddle supplements from pharma corporations.

A glass of water, drunk slowly, will cure all attacks known to science. The first thing that is offered to a person who is twisted by something terrible is a glass of water. Drinking water triggers the body's self-rehabilitation mechanism. Most often people feel sick for two reasons:

- Hysteria (sympathoadrenal crisis in another way),

- Dehydration of the body not noticed in time.

Because we don't listen to our bodies, drinking tea, coffee and sodas all day long - we all have dehydration, and you have it too. Go drink a glass of water right now and then read on.

Method 4. Get involved in an exciting, interesting endeavor.

This method is suitable in a situation when you can not "let go". It is necessary to break the stuck-on chewing "And they, And I, And yes well, all of them" something exciting, even if stupid and tasteless. Reading a detective story. A computer game. Hunting and gathering. Tracking and stalking. Trying to solve someone's mystery. Even peeping and eavesdropping, for crying out loud.

You have to be involved in the intrigue, the detective, the fast-paced action, the hunt, the game, the thrill, the flight.

Your ears should perk up and your tail should twitch.

You know what you can get excited and amused by. It's different for everyone, individual. Just don't get caught up in this stalking thing. Don't hurt anyone.

Method 5: Physical discharge.

Everyone is familiar with this method, but as usual, no one cares. And I remind you once again that rapid physical release, which includes:

- Walking on foot,
- Swim,
- General cleaning of the apartment (you can - someone else's),
- Sex,
- Junk Destruction,
- Working in the vegetable garden,
- Dance,
- Washing floors and doing laundry by hand.

Relaxes knotted muscles and relieves stress, and frustration fantastically effectively. General hand washing even helps with grief - again an old doctor's advice that I share with you.

Method 6: Make contact with water.

Washing dishes is a free hypno-psychotherapy session. The sound of clean running water relieves our fatigue and takes away all the "dirt", not only household dirt.

In addition to washing dishes, there is a well-known classic: take a bath, take a shower, go to the bathhouse, go early in the morning or in the evening - go swimming at the sea, at the river, at the lake, at the spring. Refresh yourself, in short.

Method 7: Positive reframing of stressful events.

So much has been written about positive reframing (including by me) that I don't want to repeat myself. I will just give an example:

"It's so good that it just so happens that I'm not going anywhere this summer! I'm finally going to take English classes, fitness classes, and more self-development classes! When else would I allow myself such a "useless" luxury? And in summer it's the dead season everywhere and there are only discounts all around. So, I will also save money!"

Method 8. It could be worse, it could be even harder for others.

Are you unhappy with the outcome? Imagine that there could have been a worse outcome. Imagine how bad some of the people around you are feeling. If you master this art and stop turning your nose up at this strategy, you won't need any psychotherapy at all.

Method 9: Laughter kills everything scary and scarily important.

Ridiculing, reducing, and denigrating something puffed up and important is an ancient recipe of human culture, starting from the Neolithic. Thanks to Grandpa Bakhtin for his term "carnival-mocking culture". Read it, get curious.

Or watch one episode of SpongeBob SquarePants. When he was panic-stricken about speaking at a school seminar, a clever squirrel gave him super-glasses. When he put the glasses on, SpongeBob could see all the students and the teacher... in their underwear. That was hilarious! But he never got to read his report. And the teacher's panties. Mmm.

Method 10. Count to 10.

Just read to ten. Slowly. Controlling your inhalations and exhalations. To yourself, not out loud. This is the recommendation of doctors and athletic trainers.

Method 11. Cry.

Crying relieves stress. With tear fluid, the body leaves the toxic substances that are formed under the influence of stress hormones. If you can't cry about your own, think of a pathetic topic and cry about it on purpose.

Method 12. Verbalization of everything that is on the soul.

Speaking or verbalization - putting vague "something" into clear words. It's a great thing, though. And it is even better to put it all down on paper, to write a long letter.

Just don't send him anywhere!

Here are 12 tips for dealing with anxiety disorders and the related illnesses that anxiety causes.

These 12 simple techniques that are readily available are the ones that help us and don't charge us for it.

6 effective grounding exercises for anxiety and intense emotions

When we are amid an anxiety, flashback, or panic attack, our frontal lobes stubbornly refuse to work. We feel like it's just impossible to focus or think clearly about anything, and sometimes our thoughts rush by so fast and become such a mess that it's impossible to keep track of them. We start to feel like everything around us is a blur, or when someone has been talking to us for a few minutes, we suddenly realize that we have no idea what they are talking about.

Sometimes we feel paralyzed or frozen, unable to make even the slightest movement or utter a word. This can also happen to us when we experience emotions that are too intense, such as feelings of abandonment, resentment, hopelessness, fear, or hopelessness.

Grounding techniques are a great tool for these situations and can be used wherever you are. By bringing our mind and body back to the present moment, we can organize a space for our brain to calm down and feel a little more focused, at least enough to explain what is happening to us ask for help or figure out what to do about the condition.

There are many different ways of grounding - that's why this is such a great technique - even if the techniques below don't work for you, there are many others that are worth trying to find what works for you. You can also create your grounding technique by finding what helps you focus your feelings and bring you back to the present moment.

Here are a few of my favorite grounding techniques, which I've divided into a few categories:

Complacency

1. Take a shower or bath. Focus on each step of shower/bath preparation, noticing every little detail - what does your hand feel like when you touch the doorknob and faucet? When you turn on the faucet, how do you determine the right water temperature? Note the sensations of the water on your body, paying attention to the temperature and sounds of the water, the sensations of your body muscles.

2. Find a grounding object that attracts you. It could be something like a smooth stone or a polished piece of glass, something like a ball of yarn whose texture feels comfortable to you; it could be something like a small statue or something you associate with good memories. Carry this object with you where it is easy to store and pull it out when you need to ground yourself. Pay attention to and describe in your mind every detail of the object, touching it with your hand and noting all the sensations of that touch.

3. Make a cup of tea, coffee or hot chocolate. Perform each action with the utmost mindfulness, noticing every movement your body makes; here your fingers squeeze the handle of the kettle, here your palm feels the cold of the faucet as you turn on the water, here you feel the kettle in your hand getting heavier as it fills with water. When the drink is ready, take small sips consciously, nestled in a quiet place.

Celebrate the five senses

1. Find a familiar scent (perfume, soap, lotion, tea, essential oils, etc.) and make it a habit to inhale that scent every morning, before bed, or at some other specific hour of the day.

Carry this scent with you and inhale it every time you need to ground yourself, combining this process with deep and slow breathing.

2. Put on your favorite clothing - it may be socks, a favorite sweater, or a soft, cuddly T-shirt. Note the texture, color, and smell of these clothes. A blanket or plaid will work for the same purpose.

3. Wrap yourself tightly in a blanket. Hug yourself tightly or ask someone to hug you. Rub your arms and legs, moving from bottom to top from feet to thighs, and from top to bottom from shoulders to wrists.

Use your body

1. note how your feet are on the floor. You can stand up and firmly "dig" your feet into the floor, take off your shoes, and step each foot on the ground or the floor, feeling as if your feet are the foundation of a good building, firmly connected to the ground, feeling the ground under your feet and the force of the earth's gravity. You can do this sitting on a chair or lying down.

2. (Favorite exercise!) Ground yourself. Lie down on the floor. Quickly scan your body to note exactly where the floor is touching your body, and what parts of your body are feeling it, and focus on that sensation of pressure, texture, and temperature. Note all the vibrations you can feel in the house right now. You can put a music speaker on the floor and feel its vibrations.

3. Move! Wiggle your legs, paying attention to how each leg moves separately. Try how a foot can move separately when all other parts of the body are still. Do the same with your toes, feeling the strength in your muscles, their tension, and relaxation as you move.

4. Rhythm. Tap your foot on the floor, find an object that makes a soft sound, tap your fingers on a table and quietly on glass or some other surface, find a pleasant sound, and then create a rhythm and repeat it, trying to focus on the beginning and end of each sound you create.

5. Engage in an activity that involves all parts of your body. Go to the garden to pull weeds. Try learning to knit. Buy kinetic sand or clay or something else that engages fine motor skills. Wash dishes, paying attention to physical sensations. Stack laundry neatly.

Observe your surroundings

1. Go outside (or find a window you can look through) and find any object. Note as many details of that object as you can. For example, if you chose a tree, note how light falls on it and where the branches cast their shadows. Consider whether it has many branches, buds, or leaves. Look closely at the texture of the trunk, whether the branches are straight or curved, and the shape of the leaves.

2. Slowly walk through the space you are in, try to note each contact of your foot with the ground. Note which part of your foot first touches the ground and where you feel pressure. Note how your foot comes off the ground and the moment when you are essentially balancing on one foot before you lower your foot in the next step.

3. Find something nearby that has a particular pattern and try sketching it on paper. For example, you could try sketching how the tiles on the ceiling are laid, transfer the pattern on a rug to paper, or trace the whimsical circles of the wood that make up a table.

4. Describe the room you are in now, either aloud or to yourself. If the room is too large or cluttered, you can choose a small area of the room or an object - such as a bookshelf - and note all the angles of the object, its color, light and shadows, texture, and shape.

5. If you are in a public place, look at the people around you and try to note details of their appearance. What color are their shoes? Which of them are wearing jackets? Does anyone have an umbrella or briefcase? What does their hair look like?

Distract the brain

1. Add seven to zero for as long as you get (or any other interval): zero, seven, fourteen, twenty-one, twenty-eight...

2. Play a game of "Guess the occupation". Look at the people around you and try to guess their jobs or where they are going now.

3. Think about today. Remind yourself of the date, day of the week, month, year, time of day, and where you are right now. Remind yourself that you are in this moment, not in the past, you are safe now. Note the time of year that is outside your window right now, look at what the sky looks like. Name the address where you are right now.

4. Play a game of "Categories" with yourself: choose a category, such as color, animals, or food, and try to name at least 10 objects from that category. You can also use the alphabet and try to name objects from that category for each letter of the alphabet, starting with A, B, C, etc.

5. Choose a shape (triangle, circle, square) and try to find all the objects of that shape around you. You can do the same with colors - for example, find all the green objects in the room.

Breathe.

1. Deep breathing - put one hand on your belly and the other on your chest. Breathe slowly and deeply into your abdomen, trying to make the hand on your abdomen rise as if you were inflating a balloon or balloon with air. Try not to move your hand on your chest, breathe only through your abdomen. Slowly exhale, feeling the hand on your belly descend as if you were deflating a balloon or balloon.

2. Breathing on the count of 4-7-8: slowly inhale, counting to four. Then, hold your breath for seven seconds, and at the end exhale slowly and gently for eight seconds. Repeat as many times as you feel comfortable. (Note: everyone has a different body size and lung capacity, if this particular combination doesn't work for you, you can do this exercise at intervals that are comfortable for you. The idea is that you would follow a certain pattern and your breathing would become slower).

Important note: grounding techniques are not there to get rid of unwanted emotions or to abstract from current experiences, no, they are there to give you the resources to tolerate certain experiences and emotions while staying present and present in your body. It is important to discuss these conditions with a therapist or mental health professional, especially if you notice that panic attacks, flashbacks, or dissociation have become frequent.

Treatment of anxiety disorders

If symptoms appear, it is recommended to consult a specialist. Only a doctor can recommend the right therapy for anxiety disorder based on current clinical guidelines. It may take some time to develop the right treatment plan that suits the individual patient. For most people, a combination of methods works best. Treatment is aimed at getting the patient to control and manage their emotions, not the other way around.

Treatment:

Medication treatment. Many medications can help reduce symptoms of anxiety. Pills affect the "brain chemistry" by correcting neurotransmitter imbalances. Only a doctor can choose the right treatment regimen. The drug should be taken strictly on the recommendation of a specialist. It is also important not to violate the schedule of repeated receptions and to inform the doctor about the side effects that have arisen when taking the drug.

Psychotherapy. This is a type of counseling that helps the patient learn how emotions affect their behavior. A qualified mental health professional will listen and talk about the patient's thoughts and feelings and suggest ways to understand them and cope with anxiety.

Cognitive-behavioral therapy. This common type of psychotherapy teaches the patient how to turn negative or panic-inducing thoughts and behaviors into positive ones. The patient learns how to approach frightening situations cautiously and deal with them without anxiety.

Some tips can help the patient in managing anxiety symptoms:

1. Learn as much as you can about your disorder. Do not hesitate to ask your doctor any questions you may have.
2. Adhere to the treatment plan.
3. Reduce your intake of coffee, tea, energy drinks containing caffeine.
4. Don't drink alcohol.
5. Eat right and exercise. Brisk aerobic exercise such as running, and bicycling helps fight chronic stress and improves mood.
6. Don't spare any time for sleep.
7. Learn to relax. Meditation, for example, can help with this.
8. Keep a journal. Write down your thoughts and experiences at the end of the day. You'll be surprised how much it will help you relax and fall asleep faster.

9. Manage your negative thoughts. Cognitive behavioral therapy can teach you how to redirect your thoughts.
10. Evaluate your information flows: television, radio, social media. Limit the flow of negative information and try to increase the flow of positive information.
11. Socialize more with people, and go out with friends.

Prevention

In the case of anxiety disorder, primary and secondary prevention are distinguished.

Primary prevention is aimed at preventing the development of the disorder itself. Its components are:

1. Lifestyle correction. Regular motor activity, healthy diet, and sleep patterns contribute to overall physical and psycho-emotional well-being, which reduces the risk of anxiety.
2. Avoiding stressful situations, and learning to manage emotions. Develop stress tolerance - learn to respond calmly and consciously to life's difficulties and stresses. Relaxation techniques, meditation, yoga, sports, and daily walks are usually helpful.
3. Psychotherapy. If you feel that you can not cope with some emotions, do not drive yourself to exhaustion of the nervous system. Contact a psychotherapist at the appearance of signs of anxiety, depression, or apathy. It is better to work through the problems with a specialist before they become neglected and insoluble.
4. Give up bad habits - smoking, alcohol abuse, taking psychotropic drugs. All of them badly affect the psycho-emotional background, and additionally provoke the development of pathologies of internal organs.
5. Engage in a hobby that pleases you. This will distract you from negative thoughts and help stabilize your emotional background.

Secondary prevention is aimed at preventing relapses of anxiety disorder. It includes:

- Compliance with the recommendations of the attending physician, including taking prescribed medications;
- timely referral to a psychotherapist for supportive therapy;

- Eliminating or minimizing stress;
- proper work, sleep, and rest regimen.

Psychotherapy can help you change your attitude towards reality, reduce your anxiety levels, get rid of obsessive thoughts, and look at the world more positively. Therefore, if you feel that the signs of anxiety disorder are returning, see a therapist again.

Forecast

In general, the prognosis is favorable. All types of anxiety disorders are perfectly amenable to treatment with pharmacological drugs and psychotherapy. The timing of therapy depends on the severity of clinical manifestations and the timeliness of contacting a doctor.

CHAPTER 3

MAYBE I'M DEPRESSED.

"Depression isn't a sign of weakness - it's a sign that you've been trying to be strong for too long..."

- Unknown Author

Definition of depression

Depression (clinical depression, depressive disorder) is a mental disorder characterized by pronounced apathy, pessimism, decreased mood, and activity, and loss of interest and satisfaction in activities that used to bring joy.

A complex of factors is involved in the development of depression - from genetic predisposition to severe stress. But what exactly provokes the disorder, scientists still do not know. Hippocrates defined melancholia as a disease accompanied by fear and despondency

Advice to cheer up or pull yourself together does nothing to help a depressed person, but doctors have effective therapies to get them back on track.

Depression-like states have been described as far back as Antiquity. However, at that time they were called melancholia. The point is that in ancient Greece it was believed that all diseases are caused by an imbalance of four basic body fluids, or so-called humors: blood, phlegm, yellow bile, and black bile (venous blood). According to the ancient Greeks, melancholia is a disorder related specifically to black bile.

In the 17th century, the English scientist Robert Burton described depression in detail in his work The Anatomy of Melancholy, based on numerous theories and his own experience. Burton suggested that melancholy could be combated by eating a healthy diet, getting enough sleep, music, and labor, and talking openly about the problem with a friend.

In the 20th century, German psychiatrist Emil Kraepelin first described manic-depressive psychosis and attributed the symptoms of depression to it. Later, other forms of depression were also recognized.

The term "depressive disorder" itself was introduced by a group of American scientists in the mid-1970s.

In the International Statistical Classification of Diseases and Related Health Problems, Tenth Revision, first-onset depressive disorder is coded as F32 Depressive Episode.

Depending on the form of the illness, six subgroups of depressive episodes are distinguished:

- F32.0 is a mild depressive episode.
- F32.1 is a moderate depressive episode.
- F32.2 - severe depressive episode without psychotic symptoms.
- F32.3 - severe depressive episode with psychotic symptoms.
- F32.8 - other depressive episodes.
- F32.9 - depressive episode unspecified.

According to the World Health Organization, approximately 5% of the world's population suffers from depression.

The majority of all patients with depression are women. According to experts, this may be due to regular hormonal changes in the female body.

Over the past five years, the top 5 countries in terms of depression prevalence have consistently included the US, Australia, and Brazil.

Doctors and scientists believe that such estimates are lower than the real numbers and are highly dependent on the level of medicine and the culture of seeking psychiatric care. However, even in developed countries, depression is often undetected.

The countries with the lowest prevalence of depression are the Solomon Islands, Papua New Guinea, and the Solomon Islands' "neighbor", the Republic of Vanuatu.

Causes of depression

The exact causes of depression are unknown. It is believed that depressive disorder occurs due to a complex of factors: genetic predisposition, brain disorders, severe or chronic stress, certain comorbidities, and lifestyle factors.

Hereditary predisposition

It is believed that the risk of depression is about 40% determined by genetic predisposition. Therefore, if there have been cases of depressive disorder in the family, the probability of developing pathology in blood relatives increases significantly.

Based on data from a private biotechnology company, scientists have identified specific DNA regions that are associated with depression. The company provided the researchers with biomaterial from hundreds of thousands of people, some of whom had a confirmed diagnosis of depressive disorder.

As a result, the scientists discovered two interesting genomic regions. One of them contained a poorly understood gene known only to encode a protein synthesized in the brain. The other region contained a gene that is linked to epilepsy and mental retardation, factors that increase the risk of depression. In total, scientists were able to identify 15 genes directly linked to depression.

Neurotransmitter malfunction

During depression, the production of the so-called happy hormones - the neurotransmitters serotonin, norepinephrine, and dopamine - is disrupted. With the help of these substances, brain cells exchange information with each other. Scientists still do not know exactly why this malfunction occurs.

When neurotransmitters are lacking or their balance is disturbed, symptoms characteristic of clinical depression appear apathy, joylessness, and pessimism.

Certain diseases

Depression is more common in people who suffer from chronic pathologies such as rheumatoid arthritis or disc herniation, as well as in patients with diabetes, multiple sclerosis, and cancer.

In addition, disorders of the thyroid gland and adrenal glands (hypothyroidism, hyperthyroidism, adrenal insufficiency) can provoke symptoms of depression. The fact is that in such pathologies the production of hormones is disturbed, which can affect mood and lead to irritability, increased fatigue, and apathy.

Hormonal changes

Women suffer from clinical depression on average twice as often as men. The peak incidence occurs during the reproductive period, during which the balance of female sex hormones changes several times a month. The risk of developing depression significantly decreases only after the onset of menopause. Most often depression starts during menstruation, pregnancy, and premenopausal.

Circadian rhythm disorders

Circadian rhythms, or the so-called internal clock, are physical, mental, and behavioral changes that obey a 24-hour cycle.

The main regulator of circadian rhythms is light. Normally, a person wakes up at dawn and is at the peak of energy, while at nightfall he yawns and feels tired. But if you watch soap operas at night, work the night shift, and fall asleep at first light, your circadian rhythms can become disrupted and increase your risk of developing a depressive disorder.

In winter, when the day is shorter and people go outdoors less often, the risk of disrupting the smooth functioning of the "internal clock" is doubled, so in the cold season, people are more likely to suffer from depression. Therefore, it has been proven that seasonal depression is caused by disruption of normal circadian rhythms.

Poor nutrition

Vitamin and mineral deficiencies due to a poor or monotonous diet can contribute to depression. A diet low in healthy fatty acids increases the risk of depression.

Stress

Depression can be triggered by severe stress, such as the loss of a loved one or the loss of a job. Researchers suspect this is due to high levels of the stress hormone cortisol, which can affect the neurotransmitter serotonin.

Psychoactive substances

Chronic alcohol abuse or drug use contributes to the development of a depressive disorder. Some medications, such as anticonvulsants, blood cholesterol-lowering drugs, sleeping pills, hormones, and heart medications, have the same side effects.

Organic diseases of the brain

Depression often develops after a stroke, in multiple sclerosis, malignant neoplasms, atherosclerosis, dementia, post-traumatic states, and other pathologies affecting the brain. In this case, it usually has a persistent and progressive character.

The disorder is thought to be directly related to changes in the brain that can lead to a malfunction in neurotransmitter production.

But none of these causes acts in isolation. For example, a hereditary predisposition can only increase the risk of depression, while the loss of a job or the death of a loved one can be a trigger.

Classification of depression

The disease is categorized by severity and type of course. According to the degree of severity, mild, moderate, and severe depression are distinguished. In the mild and moderate form of the disorder, a person retains the ability to work, but his quality of life is significantly reduced. In the severe form, people are unable to perform the usual activities (washing, going to work).

Depression can develop on its own or in the structure of other mental disorders.

Depending on the features of manifestations distinguish a large number of variants of depressive disorder, of which the most common are:

- melancholic - the most severe form, in which the person experiences vital longing and physical pain in the chest, neck, and head, lie in bed for days, stops talking and caring for himself;
- anxious - a person is afraid of getting a deadly disease, constantly anxious and this triggers physical manifestations (palpitations, cold sweats, digestive disorders);
- anergic - along with the classic symptoms of depression, there is a loss of emotional coloring of events, actions, statements, and thoughts.
- atypical - there are specific signs: increased appetite, weight gain, increased sleepiness; depersonalization - a person feels as if his body, environment, and mental activity have changed so much that they seem unreal, distant.
- masked - the so-called hidden depression, in which emotional manifestations are minimal, the focus is on physiological symptoms (changes in blood pressure and pulse, pain);
- hypochondriacal - manifested by constant preoccupation with their health, searching for hidden severe, incurable diseases;
- Hysterical - manifested by hyperexcitability (hand tremors, impaired coordination of movements, seizures) as well as hysterical seizures.

- apathetic - manifested by depression, anxiety, depressed emotional state, and prolonged longing.
- asthenic - begins imperceptibly, and proceeds slowly, with periods of improvement and deterioration. It is accompanied by a low mood but without feelings of sadness or guilt.

Forms of depression by type of course:

There are forms of depression according to the type of course:

1. clinical depression,
2. persistent depressive disorder,
3. bipolar disorder,
4. postpartum depression,
5. premenstrual dysphoric disorder,
6. seasonal depression,
7. atypical depression.

1. Clinical depression

Clinical depression, or major depressive disorder, is a condition in which a person feels a persistent sense of sadness, loses interest in life, and is unable to perform everyday activities.

Signs of clinical depression:

- Lack of interest in activities you used to enjoy.
- sudden weight gain or, conversely, weight loss.
- sleep disturbances;
- apathy.
- a feeling of helplessness.
- difficulty concentrating.
- thoughts of death or suicide.

If at least one of these signs persists in a person for more than 2 weeks, they should see a mental health professional as soon as possible.

2. Dysthymia (persistent depressive disorder)

Dysthymia is chronic depression that lasts more than 2 years in adults and at least 1 year in children and adolescents. It is characterized by less severe symptoms than clinical depression.

Signs of dysthymia:

- sadness,
- anger and irritability,
- low self-esteem,
- difficulty falling asleep,
- a constant urge to sleep,
- apathy,
- appetite disturbances.

Dysthymia affects women (1.9%) more often than men (1%). That is, at least 1 person in 100 has experienced a persistent depressive disorder at least once in their life.

3. Bipolar disorder

Bipolar disorder is a mental illness characterized by alternating periods of mania and depression. In the manic phase, the person feels excited, irritable, or energetic, while in the depressive phase, his or her well-being deteriorates significantly: there is indifference to usual activities, feelings of depression, and sadness. Mood swings can occur once every couple of years or several times a year.

In addition to a depressed mood and a marked decrease in interest in life, people with this form of depression often have several physical and emotional symptoms.

Signs of the depressive phase of bipolar disorder:

- apathy,
- insomnia,
- unexplained pain,

- irritability,
- increased anxiety,
- indecisiveness and disorganization.

People with bipolar disorder have a 15 times higher risk of suicide than the population average.

4. Postpartum depression

Postpartum depression is a consequence of changes in a woman's hormonal background during pregnancy and childbirth. It is much more serious than the so-called baby blues, a mild mental disorder that can occur immediately after childbirth and usually does not last more than 2 weeks.

Estrogen and progesterone (female sex hormones) levels increase several times during pregnancy and then drop dramatically after childbirth. Postpartum depression is often associated with this spike, but the exact cause of its development is not clear. Postpartum depression occurs in one in six women

Signs of postpartum depression:

- persistent bad moods or severe mood swings;
- unwillingness to go out into society, to spend time with the child;
- appetite disturbances.
- a sense of helplessness and hopelessness.
- thoughts of hurting yourself or the baby.

Without treatment, postpartum depression can last for decades, but psychotherapists have proven ways to deal with this condition - antidepressants, psychotherapeutic techniques, and hormonal medications.

5. Premenstrual dysphoric disorder

Premenstrual dysphoric disorder is a severe form of premenstrual syndrome (PMS) characterized by increased irritability, fatigue, and strong food cravings.

Signs of premenstrual dysphoric disorder:

- weakness.
- a sense of sadness.
- sudden mood swings, often with bouts of crying.
- irritability.
- inability to concentrate.

6. Seasonal depression

Seasonal depression, or seasonal affective disorder, is a form of depression that occurs in mentally healthy people when the seasons change. Seasonal depression appears with the onset of cold weather and shorter daylight hours. It can last for a long time, starting in October and ending only in April.

At the beginning and the end of the change of seasons, seasonal depression manifests itself most vividly: a person feels constant fatigue and apathy.

Seasonal depression is most often found in areas far from the equator.

7. Atypical depression

Atypical depression is a form of depressive disorder that is characterized by specific features along with typical symptoms.

Signs of atypical depression:

- Increased emotional reaction to external stimuli (hysterical laughter or inability to quiet sobs);
- tremors in the limbs.
- dizziness.
- heart rhythm disturbances (feeling that it has stopped or, on the contrary, is about to fly out of the chest);
- shortness of breath;
- excessive sweating.
- Nausea, diarrhea, constipation, and other digestive disorders.

Symptoms of depression

Scientists do not fully know how depression develops. According to the main modern hypothesis (monoamine theory), the pathology is triggered by a malfunction in the production of neurotransmitters (serotonin, dopamine, and norepinephrine).

Serotonin deficiency is manifested by increased irritability, aggression, sleep disorders, and appetite. A decrease in the concentration of norepinephrine in the neurons of the brain leads to a feeling of apathy, and difficulty in concentrating. Dopamine deficiency is manifested by a decrease in satisfaction with favorite activities or material things.

The leading symptoms of depression are prolonged low mood, decreased activity, and loss of interest in everything you used to enjoy or inspire. However, they vary depending on the severity of the depression. So, someone can not get out of bed, and someone goes to work and almost nothing gives away that inside the gaping "black hole". Sometimes people around them think about the fact that a person was depressed too late, mistaking the symptoms for whims or character traits.

For example, such a shocking tragedy was the suicide of Chester Bennington, the leader of one of the world's most popular rock bands, Linkin Park. The musician was 41 years old and had six children. Just a few days before his death, he was recording an album in the studio, walking with his family, and looked cheerful and happy. No one noticed anything disturbing in his behavior. It turned out that he had been suffering from severe depression for many years.

1. Bad mood

Typically, when depressed, a person is in a bad mood most of the day, may complain of fatigue, and may cry a lot. Depressed children and teens may seem irritable rather than sad.

2. Decreased interest

Depressed people are often said to have "lost the taste for life", they do not want anything, and the things that used to be pleasurable no longer bring pleasure. For example, foods that a person used to love now seem bland, hobbies are not exciting, he or she starts avoiding meetings with friends and relatives, and does not answer phone calls.

3. Appetite disorder

Depressed people often have a change in appetite: they either stop wanting to eat abruptly and lose weight quickly, or, on the contrary, they overeat. Patients try to compensate for the lack of pleasure mediators with the satisfaction of eating. Depressed people often "snack" on emotions, so they get fat quickly

For example, scientists followed 25,000 men and women between the ages of 19 and 55 for 11 years and found that those who had depression or anxiety disorder had significant weight changes and were more likely to be diagnosed with obesity.

4. Sleep disorders

Problems falling asleep or other sleep disturbances are present in 90% of people with depression. Typically, a person with a depressive disorder has trouble falling asleep, sleeps restlessly, and wakes up frequently. As a result, he or she wakes up in the morning feeling broken and tired.

Less often, people with depression, on the contrary, sleep too much, but despite the long period of rest, they still feel a decline in energy. Hypersomnia - unusually long sleep of 10-12 hours. It is more common in people under 30 years of age.

Sometimes it is difficult to understand why a person's sleep is disturbed because it can be both the cause of depression and its consequence.

5. Psychomotor disorders

Psychomotor abilities are human skills that combine movement and thinking, such as balance and coordination.

During depression, psychomotor abilities are impaired. As a rule, this is manifested either by increased excitability, or, conversely, inhibition (more often). Thus, a person with psychomotor agitation will show excessive activity: tapping fingers on the table, biting nails, and shaking a leg. As a rule, elements of psychomotor agitation are a sign of the anxiety component. In turn, psychomotor retardation is manifested by slow speech, thinking, and movements.

6. Chronic fatigue

Depressed people often say they don't even have the energy to get out of bed in the morning, wash their faces, and brush their teeth. And this is not an exaggeration. A person with a depressive disorder may feel physically broken all the time, right from the morning.

7. Feelings of helplessness or guilt

Depression hurts all areas of life, including how a person feels about themselves. They may feel that everything they do is pointless, they fail, they blame themselves for any failures, and constantly mentally relive failures over and over again.

Also, people with depressive disorder are more likely than others to get into co-dependent relationships because they get used to blaming themselves for everything and seem to overlook other problems with their partner.

8. Difficulty concentrating

Depressed people often have impaired memory and concentration, and have difficulty processing information and making decisions. For example, a person may spend hours wandering around the store looking for groceries, be late everywhere, forget things, and be slower at their usual work.

This is particularly pronounced in the elderly, but they and their loved ones often do not notice it or write off such difficulties as age-related cognitive decline.

9. Constant thoughts of death

A depressed person is usually not afraid of death, but on the contrary, may think a lot about it, plan ways to commit suicide, prescribe step-by-step plans, or make actual suicide attempts. Most often suicidal thoughts visit young people between the ages of 18 and 25.

Symptoms of depression by age

Bad mood, decreased activity, and loss of interest in life are common symptoms of depressive disorder in people from 20 to 50 years old. But depending on age, there are also specific signs of depression.

1. Symptoms of depression in children

Depression in children most often manifests itself as a loss of interest in favorite hobbies, stopping socializing with friends, and avoiding talking to parents. The child may abruptly refuse to go to training and other activities that he or she used to attend with pleasure, not want to go to school or stop going for walks or calling friends.

2. Symptoms of depression in adolescents

Depression in adolescents often manifests itself in the form of longing, and isolation, and there may be attempts at self-harm. They try to dull the mental discomfort with physical pain.

Usually, there is a sharp decline in academic performance, the child may openly declare that he or she sees no point in attending school, or even start skipping classes altogether. Adolescents with depressive disorder are also more likely than other children to risk their health: they start smoking, use drugs or alcohol, radically change their appearance, and refuse to take care of themselves.

3. Symptoms of depression in older adults

As we age, the functional capacity of the brain decreases. This includes the cells sensitive to pleasure mediators. In this context, depression in older people can be seen as a manifestation of brain aging.

Reluctance to leave the house and prolonged moping are the main signs of depression in the elderly. Because the elderly are usually less inclined to talk about their feelings, this symptom is often written off as age-related.

But, unfortunately, people over 70 are at increased risk of developing depression, so these symptoms should be taken seriously. The fact is that in the so-called active period of life (before retirement) people have millions of worries, tasks, and socializing, and there is simply no time to think about worries. A person feels needed and is usually clearly aware of their goals and objectives. After the end of labor activity, most people have a lot of free time, which a person simply does not know what to fill, and loved ones are either separated or busy with their lives. As a result, the elderly person is often left alone, with a depressed mood that contributes to the development of depression.

Complications of depression

People with clinical depression are more likely than others to suffer from co-occurring disorders such as increased anxiety, phobias, and somatic manifestations ("somatization of depression"). Due to the imbalance of "happy hormones" and "stress hormones", they often suffer from chronic unreasonable body pain, migraine, eating disorders, sleep disorders, and gastrointestinal problems.

But depression itself can also be a complication. For example, depressive disorder is often detected in people with chronic diseases, including those that are incurable.

What are the dangers of depression?

Depression is dangerous because a person gradually loses the instinct of self-preservation, it seems to him that if everything in life is so bad, then there is nothing to live for. Sooner or later, the persistent feeling of sadness and hopelessness makes the person think about suicide.

According to statistics, about 15% of people with a depressive disorder commit suicide. This does not take into account suicide attempts that failed to be completed. The actual number of cases can be much higher. More often than not, single people and those who have a history of suicide in their family decide to commit suicide.

Diagnosis of depression

There are no tests or examinations that can confirm or deny depression in a person. Diagnosis is made based on a face-to-face appointment and anamnesis. In addition, the doctor may ask the patient to fill out a questionnaire in which the patient has to answer questions about his or her mental health.

Laboratory and instrumental diagnostics help identify co-occurring disorders and complications of depressive disorder.

Which doctor to see if you suspect depression

Depression is diagnosed and treated by a psychiatrist, psychotherapist, and neurologist (excludes organic diseases of the nervous system). Often, especially in summarized depression, the patient requires the intervention of a multidisciplinary team of doctors.

To find verified specialists, services have been created where their contacts are aggregated and their diplomas are verified.

It is possible to consult a psychologist on the diagnosis of depression, as well as to get a second opinion from an expert on the results of the conclusions of other specialists using telemedicine consultations.

In addition, the services of psychotherapists can be obtained free of charge, for example, in psychoneurological dispensaries, departments of the service of psychological assistance to the population, or special psychotherapeutic centers of psychiatric hospitals.

Tests and questionnaires to detect depression

According to the American Psychiatric Association's Diagnostic and Statistical Manual of Mental Disorders, a diagnosis of depression can be made if a person has 5 or more of the following signs for at least 2 weeks.

Signs of depression:

- bad moods or constant irritability.
- A significant decrease in pleasure or interest in all or almost all activities.
- decrease or, conversely, increase in weight and appetite.
- insomnia or, conversely, too much sleep (more than 10 hours).
- psychomotor agitation or lethargy.
- increased fatigue.
- feelings of helplessness, guilt, worthlessness.

- difficulty concentrating.
- suicidal thoughts.

The diagnosis of clinical depression is made when the manifestations of the disorder have a significant impact on quality of life and the specialist has ruled out other conditions that may trigger depressive episodes, such as certain diseases of the nervous system or substance use.

In addition, the doctor may prescribe electroencephalography to determine the electrical activity of the brain or magnetic resonance imaging, but only if other disorders are suspected.

The Beck Depression Scale test.

The Beck Depression Inventory (Beck Depression Scale) was created by A.T. Beck, the founder of cognitive-behavioral therapy, and is based on clinical observations that identify the most significant symptoms of depression and the most common complaints of patients.

After correlating this list of parameters with the clinical descriptions of depression found in the relevant literature, a questionnaire including 21 categories of symptoms and complaints was developed.

Filling instructions

Although this questionnaire gives a probable result, you should not self-medicate after taking it and receiving the results. If you are worried about something or your test result indicates depression, you should seek qualified help from a psychotherapist or psychologist.

This questionnaire consists of 21 groups of statements. Read carefully and circle the number (0, 1, 2, or 3) of the statement that best represents how you felt during the LAST WEEK, including TODAY. If more than one statement in the group seems appropriate to you, circle each one. Make sure you read all the statements in each group before you make your choice.

I.	0	I don't feel frustrated, or sad.
	1	I'm upset.
	2	I'm frustrated all the time and can't disconnect from it.
	3	I'm so frustrated and unhappy that I can't take it.
II.	0	I'm not worried about my future.
	1	I feel puzzled about the future.
	2	I feel like there's nothing in the future for me.
	3	My future is hopeless and nothing can change for the better.
III.	0	I don't feel like a failure.
	1	I feel like I've failed more than other people.
	2	When I look back on my life, I see a lot of failures in it.
	3	I feel like as a person I'm a total failure.
IV.	0	I get as much satisfaction out of life as I used to.
	1	I don't get as much satisfaction out of life as I used to.
	2	I don't get satisfaction from anything anymore.
	3	I'm completely unsatisfied with my life and I'm bored with everything.
V.	0	I don't feel guilty about anything.
	1	Often enough, I feel guilty.
	2	I feel guilty most of the time.
	3	I feel guilty all the time.
VI.	0	I don't feel like I can be punished for anything.
	1	I feel like I could be punished.
	2	I expect that I may be punished.
	3	I feel grounded already.
VII.	0	I wasn't disappointed in myself.
	1	I was disappointed in myself.
	2	I'm disgusted with myself.
	3	I hate myself.
VIII.	0	I know I'm as good as anyone else.
	1	I criticize myself for my mistakes and weaknesses.

	2	I blame myself for my actions all the time.
	3	I blame myself for all the bad things that happen.
IX.	0	I never thought about killing myself.
	1	Thoughts of suicide come to me, but I will not carry them out.
	2	I'd like to kill myself
	3	I'd kill myself if I had the chance.
X.	0	I don't pay any more than usual.
	1	I cry more often now than I used to.
	2	Now I cry all the time.
	3	I used to be able to cry, but now I can't, even if I want to.
XI.	0	I'm no more irritable than usual right now.
	1	I get irritated more easily than I used to.
	2	Now I feel annoyed all the time.
	3	I became indifferent to things that used to annoy me.
XII.	0	I haven't lost interest in other people.
	1	I'm less interested in other people than I used to be.
	2	I've almost lost interest in other people.
	3	I completely lost interest in other people.
XIII.	0	I put off making a decision sometimes, as I have in the past.
	1	I put off making a decision more often than I used to.
	2	I have a harder time making decisions than I used to.
	3	I can't make decisions anymore.
XIV.	0	I don't feel like I look worse than usual.
	1	It worries me that I look old and unattractive.
	2	I know there have been significant changes in my appearance that make me unattractive.
	3	I know I look ugly.
XV.	0	I can work just as well as I used to.
	1	I need to make an extra effort to start doing something.
	2	I can hardly bring myself to do anything.
	3	I can't do any work at all.

XVI.	0	I sleep as well as I ever have.
	1	I'm sleeping worse now than I used to.
	2	I wake up 1-2 hours earlier and have a hard time falling asleep again.
	3	I wake up a few hours earlier than usual and can't go back to sleep.
XVII.	0	I'm no more tired than usual.
	1	Now I get tired faster than I used to.
	2	I get tired of almost everything I do.
	3	I can't do anything because I'm tired.
XVIII.	0	My appetite is no worse than usual.
	1	My appetite has gotten worse than before.
	2	My appetite is much worse now.
	3	I have no appetite at all.
XIX.	0	I haven't lost any weight lately or the weight loss has been negligible.
	1	I've lost over 2 pounds recently.
	2	I've lost over 5 pounds.
	3	I've lost over 7 pounds. I am intentionally trying to lose weight and eating less (marked with an X). YES_____ NO_____
XX.	0	I don't worry about my health any more than I usually do.
	1	I am worried about my physical health problems such as pain, upset stomach, constipation, etc.
	2	I am very concerned about my physical condition, and it's hard for me to think about anything else.
	3	I am so concerned about my physical condition that I can't think about anything else.
XXI.	0	I haven't noticed a change in my interest in sex lately.
	1	I'm less preoccupied with sex issues than I used to be.
	2	I'm much less interested in sexual issues now than I used to be.
	3	I've completely lost sexual interest.

Outcome Assessment:

0-9 - no depressive symptoms

There are no symptoms of depression. Your psycho-emotional state is normal and does not cause any concerns.

10-15 - mild depression (sub-depression)

Signs of mild depression (sub-depression). It is time to think about your mental health and consult a psychologist.

16-19 - moderate depression

Symptoms of moderate depression. Depression at this stage creates certain difficulties for normal life and is dangerous for a rapid transition to the next stage. It is necessary to seek help from a psychologist.

20-29 - severe depression (medium severity)

Signs of severe depression (moderate depression). Depression at this stage creates obstacles to normal life and can easily turn into severe depression. Such a condition should not be left without attention and medical control, it is mandatory to make an appointment for a psychologist's consultation.

30-63 - severe depression

Symptoms of severe depression. This is the last, most dangerous stage of depression, which is unlikely to be coped with alone. It is urgent to seek help from a psychologist.

It is important to note that only a professional doctor can make a diagnosis, but better and as I would recommend doing, see 2-3 unrelated specialists and only then decide if treatment is necessary.

Treatment of depression

Depression can be cured or its manifestations can be significantly reduced. Doctors use antidepressants, psychotherapy, lifestyle adjustments, physical therapy, transcranial magnetic stimulation, or a combination of these and other methods. Let's talk a little bit about each of the methods.

Antidepressants

Different classes of antidepressants are used to treat depression. They restore the balance of "happy hormones" in several ways: they selectively block some of them or change the activity of specific receptors. The most common side effects of antidepressants are nausea, decreased libido, and diarrhea.

Antidepressants are not only used to treat depression - they are also effective for anxiety, irritability, obsessive-compulsive disorder, compulsive overeating, and post-traumatic stress disorder.

Groups of antidepressants used to treat depression:

- selective serotonin reuptake inhibitors: drugs of this group are prescribed most often because they are considered the safest and usually cause minimal side effects;
- norepinephrine reuptake inhibitors selectively block the production of norepinephrine, have a psychostimulant effect, and reduce appetite;
- selective serotonin and norepinephrine reuptake inhibitors: they combine the qualities of the first two groups and have an additional anti-pain effect;
- tricyclic antidepressants are the first generation of antidepressants. They are usually used when other groups of drugs are not effective enough. They are associated with a higher risk of unwanted side effects;
- monoamine oxidase inhibitors - drugs that are prescribed only if more modern classes of drugs have proved ineffective. They have many side effects, and while taking them, it is necessary to follow a strict diet: cheese, pickles, and alcohol are excluded.

Choosing the right antidepressant is not an easy task. The fact is that such drugs have clear individual characteristics: what helped one person is not suitable for another. In addition, modern antidepressants have a dose-dependent effect: as the dosage is changed, the effect on a particular neurotransmitter is "switched on" or "switched off". You should only change the drug or its dose in consultation with your doctor. Often, to find the right antidepressant, you have to try several drugs and this is normal. We are all individualized.

In order not to waste time on the selection of a suitable antidepressant, the doctor may recommend a person's genetic tests, the results of which can immediately determine the effective drug for a particular patient.

Most antidepressants have an accumulative effect and do not start working immediately, but only a few weeks after taking the first tablet. Therefore, if a person does not feel an antidepressant effect at first, there is no need to stop taking the medication. Also at the beginning of taking some antidepressants may increase anxiety, this is due to a change in the balance of neurotransmitters. Therefore, at the start of therapy, the doctor may prescribe a "cover" in the form of an anti-anxiety drug.

Abruptly stopping treatment or skipping several doses of the medication can trigger withdrawal or worsen depression.

Psychotherapy

My favorite method used on myself. Psychotherapy is a conversational method of treatment. In the process of dialog, the specialist helps a person to change the distorted view of himself and his life, as well as to improve relationships with others and cope with stress, and fears.

Psychotherapists' approaches to treatment differ, but scientists have found that this does not affect the outcome of psychotherapy. The main thing is that sessions should be conducted by a qualified professional.

Types of psychotherapy used to treat depression:

- Interpersonal therapy focuses on relationships with other people and the problems that arise in relationships;
- Cognitive behavioral therapy helps change negative thoughts or behavior patterns that may contribute to or worsen depression.
- Psychodynamic therapy is a type of therapy in which the therapist encourages the person to say whatever is on his or her mind. This helps to realize hidden meanings and patterns and to understand unresolved inner conflicts.

Psychotherapy in the treatment of depression is used only in conjunction with treatment with antidepressants.

Instrumental methods of treatment

If a depressed person is not or is poorly helped by antidepressants and psychotherapy, if he or she cannot take medication for health reasons, or is at high risk for suicide, the doctor may additionally prescribe electroconvulsive therapy, magnetic stimulation, or vagus nerve activation.

These methods use electrical or magnetic pulses of different intensities, with the help of which the doctor manages to stimulate the activity of neurons in the brain.

Electroconvulsive therapy. During the session, electric currents are passed through the brain, which change the balance of "happy hormones" and thus promote recovery. This method of treatment shows good results, but at the word "electroconvulsive shock" most people think of scary scenes from movies where the hero is in pain.

In fact, during the electroconvulsive therapy procedure, the person is under general anesthesia and does not feel anything, and immediately afterward can go about their business, no recovery period is required. The electroconvulsive therapy procedure lasts 1 minute and the person feels no pain.

There are no absolute medical contraindications to electroconvulsive therapy. Relative contraindications are central nervous system tumors, recent myocardial infarction, and active pulmonary infection.

Electroconvulsive therapy is used if a person is not helped or is not well served by antidepressants and psychotherapy.

Transcranial magnetic stimulation. This type of therapy uses magnetic, rather than electrical, pulses to stimulate the brain. A small device is placed on the head that emits magnetic pulses. Passing through the brain's membranes, the pulse turns into an electric current and changes the functioning of the "happy hormones".

Unlike electroconvulsive therapy, a person is not under anesthesia during a magnetic stimulation procedure and may experience mild discomfort.

In addition to depression, this method is used to treat delayed speech development and attention deficit hyperactivity disorder.

Electrical stimulation of the vagus nerve. The vagus nerve is a long nerve that runs from the brain through the neck to the heart, bronchi, lungs, and digestive organs. It carries information from them to the brain and back again.

Stimulation of the vagus nerve changes its activity and leads to the release of the neurotransmitter acetylcholine, which is responsible for mental activity and mood. When acetylcholine levels are high, a person stays alert, resists stress more easily, and perceives difficulties more easily.

For this purpose, an operation is performed: a device is implanted under the left clavicle that sends regular weak electrical impulses to the brain. Stimulation of the vagus nerve helps with depression, epilepsy, and after a stroke.

Cognitive behavioral therapy for depression

Cognitive behavioral therapy (CBT) is a form of psychotherapy that focuses on how a person's thoughts, beliefs, and attitudes affect their feelings and behaviors. The American Psychiatric Association notes that CPT is based on several beliefs, including the following:

- Unproductive thinking can lead to psychological problems.
- Mastering unproductive behavioral skills also leads to psychological problems.
- People can learn productive ways of thinking and behaving.
- New habits can alleviate symptoms of mental and physical illness and allow people to be more productive.

Practitioners base cognitive behavioral therapy on the theory that problems arise from the meanings people attach to events, as well as from the same events. Unproductive emotions (sadness, despair, helplessness) and related thoughts can impair a person's confidence in various situations and ability to cope with the challenges of daily life.

One of the simplest (and at the same time very common) examples of unproductive thinking and unproductive behavior is the unwillingness to wake up in the morning and the desire to lie in bed "at least 5 more minutes". At the same time, a productive, rational approach to this problem is related to the understanding that you still have to wake up, and it is better to do it immediately after waking up, which will significantly reduce negative emotions and minimize the time of their experience.

Cognitive behavioral therapy (CBT) can have a positive impact on how people feel and act, and provides them with coping strategies that help them solve problems. Research shows that CPT can provide psychological support for people with depression, panic disorder, and other conditions. There is also growing evidence that CPT can help relieve chronic pain.

Cognitive behavioral therapy is a broad term. Different types of CBT focus on different aspects of a person's life. Some types address specific problems, such as emotional or social problems. A course of CBT consists of a series of sessions in which a doctor or psychologist and a patient or group of patients meet and collaborate regularly.

Researchers have conducted a sufficient number of studies that have confirmed the effectiveness of CPT for depressive disorders. For example, a meta-analysis of 115 studies showed that CPT is an effective treatment strategy for depression, and that combined treatment with drug therapy is significantly more effective than drug therapy alone. Evidence also indicates that relapse rates are lower in patients treated with CPT compared to patients treated with drug therapy alone. Psychological intervention is an effective and acceptable treatment strategy. It is most commonly used for mild to moderate depressive episodes. Indications for cognitive behavioral therapy include:

- The client's attitude (their faith, belief in the effectiveness of CBT for treating depression).
- Availability and accessibility of a trained therapist.
- Special situations (depression in children and adolescents, pregnancy, lactation, pregnancy planning in the reproductive age group, comorbidities, etc.).
- Impossibility of drug treatment (allergies, pronounced side effects).
- Presence of significant psychosocial factors, intrapsychic conflicts, and interpersonal problems.

At the same time, researchers note that there are no absolute contraindications to CPT. However, it is often reported that it is difficult to treat depression with CPT in patients with co-occurring severe personality disorders, such as antisocial personality disorder. Specialized training and experience may be needed to treat these patients with CPT.

In addition, researchers argue that it is difficult to achieve results with CPT alone in patients with severe depression with psychosis and/or suicidality. In such cases, special drug therapy should be administered before the use of CBT.

There is ample evidence that CPT for depression can have many benefits:

- CBT provides a reduction in symptoms of depression both as a stand-alone treatment method and in combination with appropriate medications.
- CPT provides positive changes in the patient's false ideas and beliefs that led to the development of depression.
- CBT can be used to address psychological problems of various kinds that may contribute to depression (misunderstandings and quarrels in the family, work-related stress, etc.).
- CPT reduces the likelihood of depression relapse.
- CPT improves patient adherence - patient compliance with the prescribed treatment regimen, including taking medications.

How CPT sessions work in the treatment of depression

Treatment for depression with CPT can last from ten to twenty sessions, which are usually spread out so that the patient attends sessions every week and for as many weeks as the therapist or counselor deems necessary. CPT sessions can be delivered in several ways, including:

- Face-to-face - alone with the therapist (sometimes the therapeutic conversation is also conducted over the phone).
- In a group - where the sufferer can share their thoughts with and learn from others who have similar mental health issues.
- Practice at home - in addition to individual and group therapy, patients can also do specific exercises (e.g., to overcome anxiety or fear) at home at specific times and practice these techniques in their daily lives.

A typical CPT session usually includes the following:

- Meeting with a therapist and beginning to explore the thoughts or symptoms that the patient is having problems with.

- Goal setting: what the patient wants to achieve through CPT sessions with the therapist and planning (with the therapist) the steps to achieve this goal in future sessions.
- Participating in various exercises, using charts or plans helps to understand and make sense of how the patient's thoughts relate to their emotions and behaviors.
- Practical exercises outside of sessions.
- Regular review of treatment progress and debriefing of what has been learned previously. CPT emphasizes helping people learn to be their therapists. Through exercises during sessions, as well as "homework" exercises after sessions, therapists help patients develop problem-solving skills so that they learn to change their thinking, problematic emotions, and behaviors.

An exercise from cognitive behavioral therapy for anxiety and depression:

Answer the questions in writing:

1) What bad event am I imagining? What bad thing do I imagine will happen?

_____

_____

_____

2) Looking at the situation realistically, what is the probability that this event will occur? What arguments support and refute this?

_____

_____

_____

3) If the event does happen, how bad is it? Estimate the actual probability from 0 (it's no big deal) to 10 (it's the worst thing that could happen).

_____

_____

_____

4) If the event were to occur, what thoughts (beliefs) and actions would help you cope with it? Change the situation or adapt to it.

_____

_____

_____

Perhaps as early as the second question the anxiety will decrease. It will decrease after the fourth question.

Prevention of depression

The earlier a person is diagnosed with depression and prescribed treatment, the higher the chances of a complete cure and a return to a normal life.

Without adequate treatment or if diagnosed late, depressive disorder is extremely severe and often leads to suicidal thoughts.

For example, fear of shame or judgment, reluctance to take medication, fear of going to a psychiatrist because they may be "recognized as a mental patient," "put on the register," "not issued a driver's license," or "reported for work," often cause people to hide their mental pain. Because of this, they are unable to see a doctor and get the help they need. Men are more likely to try to cope with depression on their own and not seek help.

A diagnosis of depression does not affect a person's social functions. Seeing a psychiatrist when problems arise is a normal part of health care, just like seeing a general practitioner or cardiologist for heart complaints.

Prevention of depression

If the "heaviness of mind" does not go away for more than 2 weeks, you should seek help from a psychotherapist or a psychiatrist. The main thing is not to shut yourself in.

In addition, you can try to help yourself and prevent the disease from developing.

Ways to prevent depression:

Finding a support group. Such communities bring together people with similar symptoms. As a result, the person stops feeling lonely, and the sense of collective support gives resources to cope with apathy and bad mood more quickly;

Utilizing online resources. There are enough trusted websites, chat rooms, or online programs on the Internet that are somewhat like support groups, only in an express format because they are available anytime and anywhere;

lifestyle changes. Lack of sleep, sedentary work, poor nutrition, smoking, and regular alcohol abuse deprive a person of resources to maintain normal activity: he lacks energy. As a result, the depressive state can only worsen. A varied diet, regular physical activity and 7-9 hours of sleep a day can help to avoid aggravation;

stress control. When a person is under stress, their body produces more of the hormone cortisol. In the short term, this is a good thing because it helps to gather and cope with stressful events. However, if the stress continues unabated, the person is exhausted, resulting in no strength left to overcome difficulties. Meditation, breathing practices, and outdoor walks help not to drown in emotions.

CHAPTER 4

EATING DISORDERS

"All suffering, stress, and addiction come from not realizing that you are already what you are seeking. "

- Jon Kabat-Zinn, founder of

Mindfulness-Based Stress Reduction

The concept of Eating Disorders

Eating disorders are psychiatric illnesses that damage a person's physical and mental health and impair their overall quality of life - relationships, work, and personal development suffer.

In eating disorders, the relationship with one's own body is disrupted, resulting in highly problematic eating behaviors. Weight and body shape are overemphasized, underweight is idealized, and various methods are used to lose weight or prevent weight gain.

Approximately 8% of women and 2% of men will develop an eating disorder during their lifetime. Eating disorders occur in any population, regardless of gender, age, ethnicity, or socioeconomic status. However, they are most common in girls and young women.

Eating disorders are a group of disorders that are categorized differently in different classifications. The most common eating disorders are anorexia nervosa, bulimia nervosa, and binge-eating disorder.

The term "eating disorder" is often mistakenly used synonymously with selective eating disorder because both involve eating disorders. However, the causes are different: an eating disorder is caused by a desire to control weight, while in a selective eating disorder, eating certain foods causes anxiety or fear.

Anorexia, bulimia, compulsive overeating, and other less visible eating disorders can lead to dangerous health consequences. If you suspect a disorder, you should see a doctor: medication and psychological support can completely cure most types of disorders, and in other cases - bring noticeable relief.

Eating Disorders (EDD) is a group of pathological conditions in which a person overeats, severely restricts themselves from eating, or experiences emotional discomfort due to their eating habits.

With RPP, a person may reduce the amount eaten or, conversely, eat much more than necessary, and then get rid of the "excess" by inducing vomiting immediately after eating or abusing laxatives.

It is not always possible to suspect the disorder based on a person's weight, physical shape, age, or gender: slim and outwardly perfectly healthy men, women, and even children can suffer from this pathology.

Types of eating disorders

Anorexia and bulimia are the best-known eating disorders, with movies and articles in glossy magazines. But there are many other eating disorders: avoidant (restrictive) eating disorders, compulsive overeating, and others.

Anorexia, bulimia, and compulsive overeating are the three most common and well-known eating disorders. Often, however, not all of the symptoms of a person with an eating disorder correspond to one particular disorder. In such cases, these disorders are referred to as "atypical" or "other eating disorders." It is a common myth that in such cases, the course of the disease is easier and treatment is taken more lightly. However, this is erroneous because the name of the illness only indicates its diagnostic criteria, not its severity or course.

All eating disorders, no matter what they are called or classified as are dangerous conditions that impair quality of life and require treatment.

Anorexia

Anorexia (anorexia nervosa) is an eating disorder in which a person tries to achieve the lowest possible body weight. Despite being dangerously underweight, the person feels fat and is afraid of gaining weight.

Anorexia is a mental disorder in which a person believes he or she is not slim enough, even if his or her weight is below normal. People with anorexia severely restrict their eating or exercise. This behavior leads to exhaustion and can be life-threatening. People with anorexia eat less than their body needs because they are afraid of getting fat

The pathology occurs in men and women of all ages but is most common in adolescent girls or young women.

Anorexia can be fatal - more people die from it than from other mental disorders. The main causes are exhaustion and suicide.

As a rule, the person is aware that such behavior is abnormal and is good at hiding it. People close to the person may not suspect the disorder for many years.

The disorder manifests itself in malnutrition and associated mental and physical complications. As a result of this disorder, the person eats low-calorie, often monotonous foods to avoid weight gain. The focus is on weight, appearance, and nutrition. This often becomes the main activity, negatively affecting all other important areas of a person's life. Close relationships are disturbed, and the ability to learn and work is impaired.

Anorexia usually develops in early adolescence. Young girls are most often affected. Anorexia occurs in 1% of women and 0.1% of men. Genetic predisposition to anorexia is higher than to other eating disorders. The influence of heredity on this disorder is estimated at 40-60%. Having a close relative with anorexia increases the risk of the disease by 11 times. As in all eating disorders, biological factors and environment play an important role.

Symptoms of anorexia:

- Underweight - weight is significantly lower than it should be for age, sex and height
- low body weight is caused by unhealthy behaviors: dietary restriction, excessive physical activity, intentionally induced vomiting or diarrhea, abuse of appetite suppressants or laxatives
- A distorted view of the body, perceiving yourself to be larger than you are.
- Fear of weight gain, very strict limits on your weight
- Associated hormonal, metabolic, and physical complications
- Children and adolescents have impaired normal physical development and developmental delays

Complications of anorexia:

- Decreased bone density (osteopenia, osteoporosis)
- Amenorrhea or lack of menstrual bleeding
- cardiovascular damage, arrhythmias, palpitations, decreased efficiency
- impaired kidney, liver, and pancreas function

- Gastrointestinal disorders that may involve constipation or diarrhea, abdominal bloating, abdominal pain
- damage to nails and skin, thinning of hair
- impaired thermoregulation, often accompanied by a feeling of coldness
- Chronic fatigue, weakness and loss of strength decreased tolerance to physical exertion, dizziness, shortness of breath, fainting spells
- difficulty concentrating, memory problems
- Anorexia is often associated with mood and anxiety disorders and sleep disorders

Treatment options for anorexia

Treatment for anorexia is often time-consuming and complex. People with anorexia often lack a meaningful desire for treatment as well as an understanding of the illness. Because of the strong resistance to weight gain, treatment is delayed. Thus, awareness of the disease is a prerequisite for treatment, which is facilitated by a trusting relationship between the patient and the treatment team. The main goal of treatment is to restore a regular and varied diet and thereby increase body weight. Physical observation and treatment, psychotherapy, treatment of concomitant psychiatric disorders, and involvement of family members in the patient's support are also important. Medications are not always prescribed for anorexia, but sometimes they are necessary. Treatment is often started on an outpatient basis, and in more severe cases inpatient treatment is required.

Diagnosing and treating an eating disorder usually starts with your family doctor, so if you notice any signs of anorexia, see your family doctor first.

Bulimia

Bulimia (bulimia nervosa) is an eating disorder characterized by recurrent bouts of overeating, excessive worry about one's weight, and extreme measures to control it.

Bulimia is a disorder in which a person overeats and then induces vomiting or takes laxatives without an indication to avoid gaining excess weight. Bulimia most often affects adolescents.

During bouts of overeating, large amounts of food are eaten, which are subsequently compensated for by various unhealthy behaviors: deliberate vomiting, abuse of laxatives or appetite suppressants, excessive exercise, and periodic periods of fasting. The person's thoughts revolve around food and eating, much attention is paid to weight and how to control it, the desire to lose weight, and the fear of gaining weight. The disease is characterized by a vicious cycle in which overeating is followed by guilt and regret, leading to compensatory behavior and temporary starvation, which in turn increases the likelihood of recurrent bouts of overeating. The most common age of onset is adolescence and early adulthood. The prevalence of bulimia is 1-4% of the population.

Symptoms of bulimia:

- making weight extremely important, fear of gaining weight, desire to lose weight
- during overeating episodes, the person eats significantly more food than usual in this situation, eats foods that he or she usually tries to avoid (high-calorie foods, sweets, fast food), often hides eating from others, feels a loss of control
- overeating causes shame and guilt
- compensating for the weight gain-inducing effects of the food eaten: deliberately inducing vomiting, abuse of laxatives, excessive exercise
- patients are normal or overweight, weight fluctuates widely

Complications of bulimia:

- Intentional vomiting causes burns from gastric juice that damages teeth, throat, esophagus
- frequent vomiting causes enlargement of the salivary glands, cracks in the corners of the mouth, and thickening of the skin on the knuckles.
- esophageal sphincter weakness
- Vomiting and abuse of laxatives leads to loss of electrolytes, electrolyte disturbances can lead to muscle weakness, seizures, arrhythmias

Treatment options for bulimia

Treatment for bulimia is usually started on an outpatient basis, and in more severe cases, inpatient treatment may be required. The main goal of treatment is to restore normal and varied eating and to stop the compensatory activities that are damaging to health. Attention is given to treating physical injuries and preventing further harm. Diagnosis and treatment of co-occurring psychiatric disorders are important. The use of psychotherapy or medication can be effective.

Diagnosing and treating an eating disorder usually starts with your family doctor, so if you notice any signs of bulimia, see your family doctor first.

Avoidant (restrictive) eating disorder (ARFID) is a disorder in which a person severely limits the amount of food he or she eats or completely refuses to eat a particular type of food without a medical reason. The person may exclude foods of a certain color or texture, or may have no interest in food at all. Some people refuse food because they are afraid of choking. People with this disorder do not suffer from distorted perceptions of their bodies.

ARFID develops early - often in childhood (but can occur in adults as well). It is not just a child's whimsical eating behavior: a person with this disorder does not get enough nutrients and calories, which leads to developmental delays and impaired physiological processes.

In children, a disorder can be suspected if growth is stunted and the amount of "acceptable" foods only decreases over time.

Rumination

Rumination is unintentional (unlike bulimia) regurgitation of food after eating. The condition is not associated with a disorder of the gastrointestinal tract.

In rumination, the body often receives insufficient nutritional elements. The work of systems and organs deteriorates, and immunity decreases.

The disorder usually occurs in young children or in people who suffer from mental disorders.

Compulsive overeating

Compulsive overeating disorder (binge-eating disorder) is an eating disorder in which there are bouts of overeating but no compensatory behavioral mechanisms are formed.

Compulsive overeating is regular bouts of overeating, when a person cannot stop in the process, and afterward feels physical and psychological discomfort, and scolds himself for his weak will because again he could not resist eating. A similar state can occasionally be experienced by people without eating disorders, for example, at the holiday table or on vacation, where there are a lot of appetizing new dishes. But if it happens regularly, it is said to be a disorder.

As a rule, people overeat not accidentally, plan a "belly feast" in advance, and try to eat when no one sees. Some people even have favorite dishes for gluttony.

The disorder can occur at any age but usually begins to manifest during adolescence.

Milder forms of compulsive overeating include the desire to eat without hunger, and satisfying psychological rather than physiological needs with food.

During an episode of overeating, significantly more food than usual is consumed in a short period, and the person feels a loss of control over eating. People often eat without feeling physiologically hungry until they feel discomfort. After eating, there are strong feelings of guilt, shame, and depression.

Compared to anorexia and bulimia, the disease develops at a later age and the ratio of women to men is more equal. The prevalence of compulsive overeating is 3-5% of the population.

Patients with compulsive overeating have a significantly higher incidence of obesity and more somatic diseases (cardiovascular disease, diabetes, hypertension). There is also an important association with other psychiatric disorders: patients with compulsive overeating are more likely to suffer from depression and anxiety disorders, personality disorders, and alcohol and drug abuse.

Treatment options for compulsive overeating

Treatment for compulsive overeating is usually done on an outpatient basis. The focus is on restoring normal eating habits and treating associated psychiatric disorders. It is important to add moderate physical activity. Focusing only on weight loss can complicate treatment and deepen the treatment in the long term. Psychotherapy and counseling are important, during which the person learns to accept themselves and their feelings and to regulate emotions. Medication can also be effective.

Diagnosing and treating an eating disorder usually starts with your family doctor, so if you notice any signs of compulsive overeating, see your family doctor first.

Emotional drinking

Emotional eating/overeating can also be considered a form of eating disorder. Emotional eating primarily refers to eating under the influence of negative emotions, the purpose of which is to get rid of unpleasant feelings and sensations or to temporarily dampen them.

Emotional eating is not a separate eating disorder. Emotional eating is found in both healthy people (without mental health or eating disorders) and people with eating disorders. Emotional eating is more common in women and in people who are overweight or obese.

While emotional eating is somewhat familiar to many people, it becomes a problem when food becomes the only tool that can help a person cope with their feelings. With bulimia and compulsive overeating, it is the inability to cope with strong emotions that often leads to bouts of compulsive overeating, which is one of the main manifestations of these disorders. In depression, emotional overeating can also occur, which in turn can lead to weight gain. So, while emotional overeating is not a separate eating disorder, it can contribute to the formation of an eating disorder or other mental health problem, as well as interfere with maintaining a healthy body weight.

How do you control emotional eating?

One way to control emotional eating/overeating is to learn to manage one's feelings, including accepting and recognizing them and regulating them in a way that is safe for the body. A person can accomplish this task on his or her own, but a psychologist or psychotherapist can also be consulted if necessary.

The safest way for the human body to manage its feelings includes alternative ways to cope with negative emotions - instead of eating, one can try to change one's perspective on a situation that causes strong emotions, share the problem with a friend or loved one, go for a walk, etc. It is also important to be able to distinguish negative emotions from each other because only in this way a person can learn to choose the appropriate way to manage their emotions. For example, if you are sad, it will be appropriate to ask for help from close people, and if there is a feeling of anxiety, you should try to rethink the event or do breathing exercises.

Overeating under the influence of positive emotions.

Although most people talk about overeating under the influence of negative emotions, it is known that it is not uncommon for people to overeat under the influence of positive emotions. Overeating under the influence of positive emotions is more likely to occur among men.

In general, research suggests that overeating under the influence of positive emotions is not pathological, as it is not always associated with eating disorders or mental disorders. However, frequent overeating under the influence of positive emotions can cause difficulties when trying to eat healthier foods or maintain a healthy body weight.

Disordered eating behavior

When eating behavior is disturbed, eating and related activities cause emotional or physical distress. In this case, eating becomes a problem in itself, rather than nourishing the body and mind as it should.

According to various reports, at least one sign of disordered eating can occur in half of all people.

Symptoms of disturbed eating behavior:

- most of the time the person thinks about food, eating (or not eating), weight
- Meaningless interaction with food: the person searches for recipes, reads about food and cooking, and prepares food, but does not participate in the eating experience
- following a strict diet - eating only certain foods (often low-fat, low-calorie), avoiding others (often fatty, high-calorie, low-nutrient foods, sweets, fast food, meat and other animal products).
- detailed dietary control - careful monitoring of the energy value and quantity of food, weighing of food, regular keeping of a food diary
- Creating eating rules, and rituals that are not part of normal eating behavior (e.g., cutting food into small pieces before eating, eating in a certain order, spitting it

out, crumbling or breaking it, eating very slowly or very quickly, leaving something on the plate at each meal).

- Avoid eating in public places, often even in the presence of loved ones
- frequent excuses for not eating, such as "I've already eaten", "I'm not hungry", or "I ate a lot at lunch".
- Concerns from loved ones are annoying and angry, and the person denies and downplays the problem

Orthorexia

One common form of disordered eating behavior is called orthorexia. Orthorexia is an informal term used to describe a person's tendency to engage in radical forms of eating. Orthorexia is not a stand-alone disorder, but other mental disorders such as anorexia or obsessive-compulsive disorder may be behind it.

In addition to orthorexia, there are other informal terms for patterns of disordered eating behavior.

If you recognize any of the signs of eating disorders, you can try to make changes in your eating behavior according to the nutritional guidelines. If you find it too difficult to change your eating behavior, you can see a family nurse or dietitian.

Night eating syndrome

It can be part of bulimia nervosa or compulsive overeating. In this case, "morning anorexia" (lack of appetite in the morning hours), irresistible desire to eat between dinner and bedtime, and deterioration of mood in the evening hours are common. With 4 or more such awakenings during the night hours to consume food, you should think about your nutritional status. You can start by keeping a food diary, which reflects the frequency of meals, quantity, and quality of food. If you realize that it is difficult to cope on your own, you should consult a doctor.

Causes and symptoms of eating disorders

There is never one single cause for the development of eating disorders. These are complex disorders with a combination of many factors playing a role in their development. Genetic, biological, and environmental factors always play a role. Modern societal attitudes, including diet culture and the cult of slimness, promote psychological vulnerability, which can be a fertile environment for the development of eating disorders. Probably for the same reasons, a higher incidence of eating disorders is seen in sports in which weight is important and among members of appearance-oriented professions. However, it should be emphasized that watching social media or playing a particular sport does not contribute to the development of the disease. There are many factors involved in the development of the disease that are usually beyond the individual's control. However, it is often more practical and even more important to identify the factors that maintain the disease, as changing them is associated with better treatment outcomes.

Underlying the appearance of anorexia nervosa and bulimia nervosa is the dysmorphophobia syndrome. This syndrome consists of three parts:

1. a pronounced dissatisfaction with their weight and figure;
2. obsessive thoughts that this lack of appearance affects the whole life (studies, work, relations with other people);
3. lowered mood due to thoughts of lack of appearance.

There are three broad groups of eating disorders:

1. constitutional-genetic causes (this is the type of nervous system, features of the gastrointestinal tract, endocrine system);
2. Family causes (peculiarities of upbringing in childhood and related ways of reacting to external circumstances);
3. Social environment (friends, classmates, media).

It is known that the symptoms often appear in girls and women who are commonly called "perfectionists": in their opinion, everything in their lives should be perfect, all questions should be answered immediately, and everything that happens should be under control. When for one reason or another such a girl or woman has a feeling of anxiety, she tries to determine for herself: "Why am I anxious?" And at that moment, as if by itself, the answer appears: "It is because I am fat. - Therefore," the thought continues, "if you get your weight under control, everything will be fine: you can have a career, find the right friends, get married and be happy.

It is easy to influence food intake at the initial stage and you can see the results on the scale immediately, feeling the sweetness of success. It is at this point that many fall into the trap of associating success with weight control.

The fear most often faced by adolescent girls is growing up. Anxiety during such a period is closely related to the high expectations of herself in her future life that she sets for herself, as well as those set for her by her environment. "Will I be able to cope with all these expectations, so ugly?" - the girl asks herself, standing in front of the mirror.

It is not uncommon for a girl to experience body image rejection. Before puberty, girls always gain weight naturally, because the material for estrogen production is fat, and the body produces some of it before menstruation. It is this gain that greatly affects the self-image of girls. They feel a change in the way they are treated by others and this can frighten them, causing them to feel the need to develop some sort of defense for themselves. This can lead to a desire to be small again, to go back to childhood. The "new" female body is not accepted, and they want to punish and discipline it.

It is important to realize that these girls are often highly sensitive to emotions, and a level of anxiety that may be unpleasant but manageable for others may feel unbearable to them. Therefore, a special role in the development of eating disorders is played by a disabling environment - close people who do not validate the emotions experienced by the person themselves. While the person is anxious, his relatives and friends respond that it is all his fantasies or whims, but everything is fine and there is nothing to be sad about. As a result, the person begins to experience secondary emotions: shame, a sense of inferiority ("everyone is having fun, but I am sad"), resentment, and irritation ("Why do I have such feelings when I should be having fun?"). The situation becomes even more difficult if there is someone in the family who is worse off physically ("How come my sister is sick and I feel bad - I must be a terrible person"). As a result, there is an escalation of unpleasant emotions, and if initially, the person had only anxiety, then as a result it is joined by shame, guilt, a sense of one's inadequacy, resentment, anger, and irritation. The level of negative emotions grows to such an extent that it is intolerably difficult to bear them.

Eating is just such a simple and accessible momentary way to distract oneself from heavy emotions. When a person eats, his attention is focused only on this process, and as a result, there is a kind of emotional anesthesia. But this method is ineffective for relieving anxiety and guilt, because as soon as a person stops eating, all his negative feelings return, as well as added shame and a sense of loss of control. To regain control, the person performs compensatory actions: starving, vomiting, taking diuretics, and so on, and as a result, the cycle of bulimia nervosa closes.

An underlying cause of eating disorders is also the desire to boost one's self-esteem ("I'm good, I can hold back and not eat"). This is another trap a person can fall into, as this illusion of achievement and strength is hard to give up. Raising self-esteem in this way, by belittling all those "insignificant eaters" around him, leads to painful loneliness.

Symptoms. How do you know if a person has an eating disorder?

With an eating disorder, the symptoms can vary widely. A person may know they are sick (and successfully hide it from loved ones), or they may not even realize that their eating behavior is abnormal and requires medical attention. Several signs can help to identify the disorder and realize that it is time to see a doctor:

- Strictly restricting food in terms of calories, volume of food eaten, or "allowed" foods permanently.
- A fixation on your weight and fitness.
- A fixation on food and eating habits.
- Dietary restriction (avoidance of certain foods or food groups without medical reasons) that progresses over time;
- Avoiding events where there will be treats.
- Abuse of laxatives, provoking vomiting after eating.
- grueling hours of training outside of athletic competition preparation.
- Emotional instability caused by eating or refusing certain foods.

A person may not realize that their eating behavior is detrimental to their health. Some signs indicate that the body is not working properly.

Symptoms that may manifest:

- weakness, fatigue
- swelling of the face, and torso
- pain or numbness in the extremities, cramping
- cold palms and feet
- sensitivity to cold
- rapid heartbeat
- pre-syncope or fainting spells
- digestive disorders - bloating, flatulence, diarrhea, or constipation
- loss of interest in food
- menstrual irregularities
- infertility
- decreased sex drive
- delayed sexual development
- hair thinning
- overweight or underweight

It can be even more difficult to recognize an eating disorder in a loved one: people are often ashamed of their behavior and are careful to hide it from others. There are a few signs that a loved one is suffering from an eating disorder.

Signs of a Covert Eating Disorder:

- to eat a lot and fast;
- eat too little, try to avoid family meals, and even eat dinner alone;
- lying about what and how much they have eaten, such as discreetly throwing away food or, conversely, stocking up on food in secret from others;
- locking yourself in the bathroom or toilet after eating;

- to lose or gain weight dramatically;
- to have hoarseness of voice;
- having non-healing abrasions or bruises around the joints of the hand and fingers (Russell's sign). Non-healing marks on the knuckles of the hands (Russell's signs) are a sign of bulimia. Injuries occur from contact with the teeth when a person vomits

One of the indirect signs that a person suffers from PPD is that he or she eats a lot, but does not gain weight. This alone does not indicate a disorder: it is possible in healthy people with a good metabolism. But when combined with one or more of the factors listed above, it may indicate that the person needs help.

Causes of eating disorder development

The mechanism of RPP development is not fully understood. It is known that the pathology develops in people with a genetic predisposition against the background of unfavorable social factors. The disorder may be based on physiological and psychiatric disorders.

Physiological disorders

Diets that involve very strict food restrictions can lead to breakdowns and disruption of physiological processes. For example, rapid weight loss reduces the level of the hormone leptin, which controls energy stores. The brain perceives this as a life-threatening condition and demands to eat more. Also, food restriction leads to lower levels of serotonin, the hormone responsible for a person's emotional state. Anxiety and dissatisfaction with oneself can lead to overeating and eating disorders.

Psychological disorders

Psychological traits and disorders such as low self-esteem, perfectionism, anxiety, and dissatisfaction with one's achievements or life in general can lead to RPP. Some people seek comfort in food and try to compensate for missing emotions, while others look critically at their bodies and strive for perfection by severely restricting themselves.

Heredity and family traditions

Eating disorders often occur in patients' immediate family members. This may be due to genetic predisposition and behavioral patterns in the family. For example, a mom who is unhappy with her body is likely to grow up to have a daughter who is just as unaccepting of herself. This is because she either sees her mother's example or constantly hears her mother criticize her.

Social influence

Societal norms influence how people perceive their bodies and how they eat. Eating behavior can be influenced by feelings of distress about being overweight or underweight and an externally reinforced desire to change one's body to conform to societal standards.

Complications of an eating disorder

Depending on the type and course of the eating disorder, complications can range from mild to life-threatening. Many of the pathologies caused by an eating disorder may simply be overlooked (or not associated with eating habits).

Possible complications of eating disorders:
- obesity;
- diabetes;
- edema;
- digestive disorders - constipation, diarrhea;
- exhaustion;
- iron deficiency anemia;
- deterioration of teeth;
- tooth loss;
- hair loss (alopecia);
- menstrual disorders, including cessation of menstruation (amenorrhea);
- Polycystic ovary syndrome (PCOS);
- Vitamin and mineral deficiencies (e.g., scurvy, a disease caused by pathological deficiency of vitamin C);
- heart and brain dysfunction;

- kidney dysfunction;
- destruction of bone tissue (osteoporosis);
- nerve fiber die-off;
- depression, suicidal thoughts.
- Female pattern baldness. Eating disorders can provoke many complications, including alopecia (baldness).

Diagnosis of an eating disorder

The first step is to recognize the problem. People can go years without seeking medical help because they do not even recognize the signs of PPD. This may be due to underestimating the seriousness of the situation, believing that it cannot be changed, or fear of judgment. If you have symptoms of RPP, make an appointment with a therapist.

How are eating disorders diagnosed?

Because eating disorders can be very serious, it is important to seek help if you or a loved one thinks you may have a problem. Your doctor can use many tools to make a diagnosis:

-A medical history that includes questions about your symptoms. It is important to be honest about your eating and exercise behaviors so your provider can help you.

-Physical exam

-Blood or urine tests to rule out other possible causes of your symptoms.

-Other tests to see if you have other health problems caused by the eating disorder. These may include kidney function tests and an EKG (electrocardiogram or ECG).

The diagnosis is made by a psychiatric specialist based on a careful analysis of the patient's clinical history. This applies to common and rare forms of eating disorders. The doctor conducts an initial assessment and refers the patient for consultation with subspecialists, such as a gastroenterologist, endocrinologist, psychologist, and nutritionist. This approach allows for a more in-depth examination of the multifaceted nature of the problem and the development of a comprehensive treatment plan, taking into account both the physical and psychological aspects of the disease.

The psychiatrist will conduct an initial assessment and take a history to evaluate for signs of eating disorders. It will be necessary to talk about lifestyle, chronic illnesses, and any complaints. Questionnaires, questionnaires, and psychological tests are used to identify the specific subtype.

Laboratory diagnostics are also important:

- clinical blood work;
- glucose and B vitamin levels;
- ECG with transcripts;
- Ultrasound of the GI tract, peritoneum, urinary and genital systems.

Laboratory tests can be used for a more detailed assessment of the body and to clarify the diagnosis. The doctor may additionally send for several manipulations and consultations with other specialists.

Tests to detect signs of an eating disorder

For self-diagnosis at home, I suggest taking a few tests. It is important to remember that the information obtained is not decisive, but can help to find a solution, for example, in cases when all attempts to lose weight have been unsuccessful. Perhaps it is necessary to dig deeper and try to find a solution in the psychological plane. It happens that a person does not eat anything, but the weight does not go away. Another situation, about which we wrote above, is when overeating is compulsive and associated with the experience of unpleasant emotions.

Eating Attitudes Test (EAT)

The most popular test methodology for assessing the likelihood of anorexia nervosa and bulimia nervosa. It is used in many studies of eating disorders.

The EAT-26 should be used as the first step in the two-step process of diagnosing anorexia or bulimia. **A score greater than 20 indicates an increased risk of an eating disorder.** This test should not be used instead of professional diagnosis or counseling.

In addition to the test, your likelihood of having RPP is increased if you have had at least one of the following in the past 6 months:

- You've been binge eating, feeling like you can't stop.
- You induced vomiting to control your figure.
- You have used laxatives, diuretics, or specialty products to control your figure
- You spent more than 60 minutes of exercise every day to control your figure
- You've lost over nine pounds
- Your BMI is lower than normal

Anorexia/Bulimia Test Instructions

Please read the statements below and mark on each line the answer that most closely matches your opinion. All test questions, except question 26, are scored as follows: "always" - 3; "as a rule" - 2; "quite often" - 1; "sometimes" - 0; "rarely" - 0; "never" - 0. Question 26 is rated as follows: "always" - 0; "as a rule" - 0; "quite often" - 0; "sometimes" - 1; "rarely" - 2; "never" - 3.

		Never	Rarely	Sometimes	Quite Often	As a rule	Always
1	It scares me to think about getting fat.	0	0	0	1	2	3
2	I refrain from eating when I'm hungry.	0	0	0	1	2	3
3	I find myself consumed with thoughts of food.	0	0	0	1	2	3
4	I have bouts of uncontrollable binge eating during which I can't stop myself	0	0	0	1	2	3

5	I divide my food into small pieces.	0	0	0	1	2	3
6	I know how many calories are in the food I eat	0	0	0	1	2	3
7	I particularly refrain from foods high in carbohydrates (bread, rice, potatoes)	0	0	0	1	2	3
8	I feel that those around me would prefer that I eat more(a)	0	0	0	1	2	3
9	I throw up after eating	0	0	0	1	2	3
10	I experience a heightened sense of guilt after eating.	0	0	0	1	2	3
11	I'm concerned about losing weight.	0	0	0	1	2	3
12	When I exercise, I think I'm burning calories	0	0	0	1	2	3
13	People around me think I'm too skinny.	0	0	0	1	2	3
14	I am preoccupied with thinking about my body fat.	0	0	0	1	2	3
15	It takes me longer to eat a meal than it does other people	0	0	0	1	2	3
16	I abstain from foods containing sugar	0	0	0	1	2	3

17	I eat diet foods	0	0	0	1	2	3
18	I feel like food-related issues control my life	0	0	0	1	2	3
19	I have self-control when it comes to food-related issues	0	0	0	1	2	3
20	I feel pressured by those around me to eat(a)	0	0	0	1	2	3
21	I spend too much time on food-related issues	0	0	0	1	2	3
22	I feel discomfort after eating sweets	0	0	0	1	2	3
23	I'm on a diet	0	0	0	1	2	3
24	I like the feeling of an empty stomach	0	0	0	1	2	3
25	After I eat, I have an impulsive urge to throw it up.	0	0	0	1	2	3
26	I enjoy trying new and tasty dishes	0	0	0	1	2	3

If the total score of the scale exceeds the value of 20, there is a high probability of an eating disorder. However, the EAT-26 test is not a stand-alone diagnostic tool but is used for screening and preliminary assessment. If you receive a score greater than 20 or match one of the 6 items above, consult a professional.

Dutch Eating Behavior Questionnaire (DEBQ)

Quite often we cannot understand where the causes of overeating or overweight are. The Dutch Eating Behavior Questionnaire (DEBQ) can help us to understand this situation.

This questionnaire, developed by Dutch scientists in 1986, allows you to identify your type of eating behavior and the causes associated with eating disorders and overweight. The main causes are three. The first - is regular restrictions of yourself in food, increased control of your desires, and struggle with weight, and appetite, the result is many diets with constant breakdowns (restrictive eating behavior). The second - is the habit of eating emotions, food is a way to calm the emotional state. The third is the desire to severely restrict oneself in eating (externalized eating behavior). By taking the quiz (it only takes 10 minutes), you'll know what causes you to overeat and you'll be able to understand what you need to do to solve it. Regardless of the type, almost all causes of poor eating, and overweight are psychological and an eating behavior psychologist can help you change any deviation in your eating or weight.

How to take the test

Take the test quickly, without thinking about the answer. For each question, answer "never", "very rarely", "sometimes", "often", or "very often". Add up your score: "never" - 1, "very rarely" - 2, "sometimes" - 3, "often" - 4, "very often" - 5 (with 31 questions, it is the other way around). Add up the scores for the first ten questions and divide the resulting sum by ten. Add up the scores for questions 11-23 and divide the sum by thirteen. Add the scores for questions 24-33 and divide the sum by ten.

Instructions: You are asked a series of questions about eating behaviors. Answer them with one of five possible answers: **"never," "rarely," "sometimes," "often," and "very often.**

	Never	Rarely	Sometimes	Often	Very often
1. If your weight starts to gain, are you eating less than usual?	1	2	3	4	5
2. Do you try to eat less than you would like during your normal meals?	1	2	3	4	5

3. Do you often refuse to eat or drink because you are worried about your weight?	1	2	3	4	5
4. do you carefully control the amount you eat?	1	2	3	4	5
5. Do you make deliberate food choices to lose weight?	1	2	3	4	5
6. If you overeat, will you eat less the next day?	1	2	3	4	5
7. Do you try to eat less to avoid gaining weight?	1	2	3	4	5
8. Do you often try not to eat between regular meals because you are watching your weight?	1	2	3	4	5
9. Do you often try not to eat in the evening because you are watching your weight?	1	2	3	4	5
10. Does your weight matter when you eat?	1	2	3	4	5
11. Do you feel the urge to eat when you are irritated?	1	2	3	4	5
12. Do you feel the urge to eat when you have nothing to do?	1	2	3	4	5
13. Do you feel the urge to eat when you are depressed or discouraged?	1	2	3	4	5
14. Do you feel the urge to eat when you are lonely?	1	2	3	4	5
15. Do you feel the urge to eat when someone has let you down?	1	2	3	4	5
16. Do you feel the urge to eat when something obstructs you, gets in your way, or when your plans are disrupted or something fails?	1	2	3	4	5
17. Do you feel the urge to eat when you anticipate any unpleasantness?	1	2	3	4	5

18. Do you feel the urge to eat when you are anxious, worried, or tense?	1	2	3	4	5
19. Do you feel the urge to eat when "everything is wrong", or "everything is falling apart"?	1	2	3	4	5
20. Do you feel the urge to eat when you are frightened?	1	2	3	4	5
21. Do you feel the urge to eat when you are disappointed, or when your hopes are dashed?	1	2	3	4	5
22. Do you feel the urge to eat when you are excited, or upset?	1	2	3	4	5
23. Do you feel the urge to eat when you are bored, tired, or restless?	1	2	3	4	5
24. Do you eat more than usual when the food tastes good?	1	2	3	4	5
25. If the food looks good and smells good, do you eat more than usual?	1	2	3	4	5
26. If you see delicious food and smell it, do you eat more than usual?	1	2	3	4	5
27. If you have something tasty, will you eat it immediately?	1	2	3	4	5
28. If you pass by a bakery (pastry shop), do you want to buy something tasty?	1	2	3	4	5
29. If you pass by a snack bar or cafe, do you want to buy something tasty?	1	2	3	4	5
30. If you see others eating, do you feel the urge to eat?	1	2	3	4	5
31. Can you stop if you eat something tasty?	5	4	3	2	1
32. Do you eat more than usual in company (when others are eating)?	1	2	3	4	5
33. When you prepare food, do you often taste it?	1	2	3	4	5

Answers to the first 10 questions define **restrictive eating behavior. The** average score is **2.4.** If your score is much lower, it means that you have poor control over what you eat and how much you eat. If it's much higher, you're being too hard on yourself and may be inclined to seek out rigid diets. Eating with an inflated index of this type is accompanied by stress, which affects your health. Depending on how elevated you score on this type of eating behavior, so try to find more acceptable ways of weight loss alternatives to control and restriction. Relaxing exercises, pleasant music, and eating in a quiet environment can help reduce control and make eating more natural.

Questions 11-23 determine **emotional eating behavior**: how much of your eating behavior is related to your emotions. The lower the number, the less the causes of excess weight are in the emotional sphere of your life (the average score is **1.8**). If the result is high, then you have an opportunity to begin to understand when you are eating stress, resentment, anger, and other negative emotions. Try to find alternative ways to deal with your emotions, for example: when you want to eat because of your emotions, drink a glass of water, take a walk in the fresh air, or draw your anger, resentment, or grudge. Or talk to the person you are angry with.

A severely low score reflects repressed and blocked emotions. The cause may also be in your past, perhaps you once made a decision not to feel negative emotions. Reduced emotionality can also be the cause of difficulties in accepting your body, discovering your sexuality, and in relationships with your partner.

The last ten questions make up the **Externalized Eating Behavior** Scale. **The** extent to which you are tempted to eat something tasty, responding to external temptations. Here is the relationship between eating behavior in "see-want-to-eat". The average score on this scale is **2.7.** If your score is much higher, you are predisposed to external food stimuli: seen, heard, smelled and it becomes difficult to refuse. To normalize eating behavior, try to monitor yourself in these situations. It is better of course to refuse food that attracts your attention: do not keep it at home in a prominent place sweet, candy, let if it really should be in your house, it will be in the closet.

Eating disorder treatment

Treatment of an eating disorder (ED) depends on its clinical picture and type. Therapy involves a combined approach: combining medication with psychological support. In more serious cases, when the signs and symptoms of eating disorders are significant, hospitalization in a psychiatric clinic or rehabilitation center may be required. The doctor may prescribe medications: antidepressants, neuroleptics, (selective serotonin reuptake inhibitors).

Eating disorder treatment plans are tailored to meet individual needs. You will likely be helped by a team of providers, including doctors, dietitians, nurses, and therapists. Treatment may include:

- **Individual, group, and/or family psychotherapy.** Individual therapy may include cognitive-behavioral approaches to help you identify and change negative and unhelpful thoughts. It can also help you develop coping skills and change behavior patterns.
- **Medical care and supervision,** including treatment for complications that may cause eating disorders
- **Nutrition counseling.** Doctors, nurses, and counselors can help you eat right to reach and maintain a healthy weight.
- **Medications** like antidepressants, neuroleptics, or mood stabilizers can help treat some eating disorders. Medications can also help with symptoms of depression and anxiety that often accompany eating disorders.

Some people with serious eating disorders may need hospitalization or a residential treatment program. Residential treatment programs combine residential and treatment services.

It should be realized that the effect of medication may be temporary and symptoms may return after discontinuation. Therefore, treatment is supplemented with individual or group psychotherapy. If there is excess weight, a nutritionist is involved, who develops an optimal diet tailored to the patient's needs.

Treatment of RPP depends on the type of disorder and its severity. As a rule, drug therapy, and work with a psychologist are combined. In more severe cases, treatment in a psychiatric clinic or rehabilitation center is recommended.

Among medications, the doctor may prescribe antidepressants, drugs that normalize the production and absorption of serotonin, eliminating the imbalance of dopamine (neuroleptics). At the same time, the effect of drugs can be temporary - after their withdrawal often occur relapses. Therefore, it is recommended to combine drug therapy with personal, family, or group psychotherapy.

If the RPT is associated with excess weight, working with a dietitian - a doctor who selects a diet for the treatment of certain diseases - can have a good effect. In this case, the weight loss process is gentle, and the risk of failure is much lower than when trying to lose extra pounds on your own.

In addition to primary therapy, treatment of complications from the disorder may be required, such as restoring internal organ function or replenishing deficiencies.

Recovery from an eating disorder is real, but it can take a long time. It is important to start treatment as early as possible because some types of eating disorders can lead to suicide, death from exhaustion, and serious systemic and organ dysfunction.

Psychotherapy for eating disorders

Eating disorders are treated holistically. One of the main methods is adapted cognitive behavioral therapy (CBT). It helps to identify the negative thoughts associated with the eating disorder and teaches the patient to deal with them by replacing them with constructive and positive beliefs.

People subject themselves to strict diets, focusing on weight and body shape, which can increase vulnerability to emotional swings and impulsive behaviors. This leads to periods of excessive eating, followed by attempts to cleanse the GI tract to offset the effects of overeating.

Cognitive behavioral therapy is effective in treating eating disorders such as anorexia. Other methods of psychotherapy: family therapy, arts-based methods, and participation in self-help groups can also be used in conjunction with or independent of the cognitive approach.

In severe cases, hospitalization may be required if life and health are threatened. This is usually caused by physical exhaustion or serious organ problems. Treatment of eating disorders is facilitated by seeking medical attention promptly.

Cognitive-behavioral therapy exercises

As you can imagine, there can be many reasons for an eating disorder. There are no standard answers as well as life situations. If you come to see a psychologist, then depending on the method of work of the specialist you will be offered to do the most important thing, to understand the causes. After all, having understood the mechanism as an internal computer program, those who are engaged in programming will understand, that you will be able to move in the right direction. Understanding the causes of eating behavior disorder takes as a rule not one and not two sessions with a psychologist. Sometimes people who have realized the causes of their troubles see healing over time. Sometimes psychology works like this: it is important to understand the cause and as a consequence, healing occurs.

I offer you a methodology that will help you save a lot of money at least on self-analysis, with which you can come to see a psychologist and already engage in correction, or you can move on your own. The main thing is to have a result. The most important criterion is to feel good and happy.

So, what I want to show you. The logic is very simple, no special knowledge or skills are required. The main thing is your desire to solve the problem, to find its root. Motivation only from you and no one else will help you to adjust your eating habits and change your life for the better.

I can share my story and how I came to normalize my weight. In my family, it is not customary to talk about your feelings and experiences. Everything bad and good was either tabooed or expressed through tears or silence. Praise was very rare and mostly only for the cause. If you got a good mark at school - well done, if not, then there was nothing to praise. So it was customary to show my love and care for my family through food. Food became a symbol of warmth, love, care, and attention, and also an integral part of entertainment.

As an adult, food helped me to overcome depression, helped me in difficult moments, and gave me a feeling of protection, safety, and love. As soon as something happened, my hand would immediately reach for junk food. Being overweight was always present in my life. Being at an older age I began to notice swelling, especially after the weekend, which was usually spent on the couch with a plate of something tasty. Or rather with plates of...

When I accidentally stumbled upon the training and began to realize that this situation was not normal and that it was possible to live differently, I began to look for a solution. At that time, right after my divorce from my first husband, I did not have much money, and even less for such a luxury as a psychologist. This is first of all. Secondly, it was not clear where to look for them, and in general, to recognize their psychological deviations, as at the time I thought it was not easy. And in general, what my relatives and my acquaintances would say. They wouldn't understand.

So I started reading, started taking training, and started looking for tools to help me. I had no idea at the time that food symbolizes love in my life and plays an incredibly important role in my life.

So, the scheme is as follows:

		Action	Purpose
1.		Start keeping a diary of your eating habits. An example of a Food Habits diary is shown below.	**Analyze and understand what food and how much you eat in a day.** Such a diary should be kept long enough because seasonal holidays, which are usually accompanied by rich feasts do not happen every day and you should be ready for them.

2.	Keep an emotion journal along with it. An example of an emotional diary is shown below.	**Find the automatic thoughts**
3.	Analyze. Carve out time at least once a week, take the information from the two diaries, and see the patterns. Pay attention to those days where deviations are recorded and see what events or emotions accompanied them. These very emotions are extremely important and the very material with which you can further work.	**Find the triggers** that most often cause you to overeat or starve yourself. These triggers can be people, or events, even the smallest and most insignificant details are important.
4.	Highlight the arguments for and against your feelings. Think of all feelings as ones that are trying to protect you and keep you safe. Remember, behind every emotion you have is a positive intention. Always positive. Look at the pros and cons of feelings, thoughts, and reactions.	**Acceptance of irrational thoughts** and reactions. Search for hidden benefits and motives.
5.	Repetition of affirmations and rational judgments. Understanding the situation through metaphors, and parables. Working with images - transforming into neutral and then into positive.	**Replace irrational thoughts and reactions with rational ones.** Form positive thoughts.
6.	Repeating a new positive experience.	**Reinforce positive habits** and automatize them

The most important rule is to be honest with yourself. Do not try to distort or improve the information, the only person you are accountable to is yourself. You must not show anyone what you write down. This information is strictly confidential. You can show the collected data to your therapist, but as a rule, you are not asked to do so and it will be enough that you tell what you want to tell yourself. So be honest with yourself. If you ate for example a kilogram of chicken at one time, ate a whole cake for dinner, there is nothing terrible and shameful. Understand that you will write it down and will be the first step to establish eating behavior. After all, behind every action there is a motive and our goal is to figure it all out. Be your detective, get on your side.

One more important point. A lot of different applications will offer you to keep diaries online for an extra amount of money. I don't recommend using them, or you can use them, but only in addition. Realize that the fact that you find the strength to sit down, pick up a pencil, and write out reinforces your habit, it is important to use your motor skills and do everything with your hands. Also, while you are writing, you are thinking and this information is automatically processed in your brain, which is not the case with a lighter program. Make an effort in the beginning, but then it will get easier and when you see the first results, you will realize how life changes for the better. How the world around you is changing! Because your view of the world will change! I believe that you will succeed because I once succeeded.

Food Habits Diary

Date _____						
Time	**Products**	**Grams per serving**	**Kcal per serving**	**Where**	**With whom**	**Mood**

Let's look at an example of filling out a one-day food behavior diary using my example:

Date 7.10.2023						
Time	**Products**	**Grams per serving**	**Kcal per serving**	**Where**	**With whom**	**Mood**
Morning 7:00	Yogurt	300	200	At home in the kitchen	Sama	Tired, right after waking up, I'm afraid I'm gonna be late
	Honey	60	80			
	Oat flakes	100	300			
	Coffee and cream	300	50			
Morning 9:00	Meat	100	60	In the office at the desk	Sama	Anxious, had lots of tasks to do, and had a busy meeting, trying to recover
	Bun	200	400			
	Ketchup	10	25			
	Snickers	100	450			
	Coffee	300	50			
Lunch 12.00	Cookies	200	700	In the kitchen	With a coworker	It was a treat, I didn't feel comfortable saying no, but I tried to like it.
	Coffee	300	50			

Let's look at the most universal technique, the cognitive-behavioral therapy diary. Or the ABC technique, where A is an event, B is a perception, and C is a reaction. If you want to change your behavioral or emotional reactions to certain situations and events, you need to work on perception, that is, to find and change automatic thoughts.

A special table to fill in will help. Let's get acquainted with the example of cognitive-behavioral therapy for eating disorders.

Emotion Diary :

Situation	Thought	Emotions	Reactions (actions, inactions)
Criticism from the boss	It's not fair, I do more than others. I want to quit, but I can't There's something wrong with me	Anger Anger Fear of dismissal Apathy Despair	I feel warm in my body, my face turns red, my heart beats fast, my jaw clenches, I want to speak out but hold back, my attention is scattered, I can't do anything, I'm looking for a way to calm myself down, I'm thinking about chocolate bars

And here's what happens if you replace thought with rational thought:

Situation	Thought	Emotions	Reactions (actions, inactions)
Criticism from the boss	My boss's opinion is just my boss's opinion. I'm fine, I don't have to be liked by everyone. Just because he told me doesn't mean I'm bad, it means some part of my work needs correction. I will pay attention to this aspect next time. At the very least, I can always find a new job.	Calmness, slight dissatisfaction with the situation, a sense of security	I just keep going about my business

The technique can be used to work through situations from any sphere: work, personal life, family, and relationships with yourself. The main thing is to remember the essence: if you change your thoughts about what is happening, your reactions to it will change. For example, you will stop yelling at the child, if you see that the basis of such behavior - the thought "I am a bad mother", and replace it with "I am a good mother, but I have not yet found an approach to the child. I'll try again."

Over time, such thoughts become automatic, and writing them out is not necessary. Everything happens much faster in your head. That's how thinking changes.

Eating disorder prevention

It aims to support the healthy growth and development of children. Early detection of PPD significantly increases the chances of successful treatment. Proper information on topics related to appearance and body, correcting misconceptions, and avoiding misunderstandings are necessary to prevent the risk of the disease.

As part of prevention, talk to your child about the following:
1. Emphasize the importance of communicating your feelings with your loved ones, explain the need to share, and not eat up stressful situations.
2. Emphasize that estimating other people's body size and weight is incorrect.
3. Teach an understanding of body sensations, including that once satiated - you should stop eating. Good eating behavior is important.
4. Inform about normal physiologic changes in the body.
5. Focus on regular physical activity and a balanced diet.

This will help prevent the possibility of an eating disorder for your child. At the same time, you should observe the behavior closely and talk if there is any problem. Signs of a psychological eating disorder should be a reason to see a therapist for counseling.

Prevention of eating disorders in adults:
- improve stress tolerance;
- beginning with childhood to form the right attitude toward appearance and food;
- learn how to get rid of tension and the consequences of stress through sport or creativity, how to defend their point of view, and how to resolve conflicts correctly;
- avoid using food as entertainment and maximize pleasure resources.

CHAPTER 5

SOCIAL ANXIETY DISORDER

"Listen to yourself. If sadness comes to you, don't chase it away. Sit it beside you and listen to what it wants to tell you."

- Carl Gustav Jung, Psychoanalyst.

The concept of Social phobia

Social phobia, or social phobia, is a disorder that is expressed in the fear of interacting with people. The trigger for anxiety can be almost any action in which there is a risk of communication: talking on the phone, public speaking, taking an exam, or going to the store. Who are people with social phobia, what are the signs and causes of social anxiety disorder and how to get rid of it, we tell you in Forbes Life.

Social phobia is expressed by the fear of any interaction with society: socializing with people, visiting public places, and public restaurants. This condition can be described as a fear of attention to one's person, caused by the fear of negative evaluation. Therefore, people with social phobia try to avoid situations in which they might be the center of attention.

This disorder makes it very difficult to perform everyday activities: studying, working, traveling in public places, and transportation. As a result, the quality of life suffers. The person has difficulties with his or her development and realization of abilities and desires.

Social phobia is often confused with shyness, but these two concepts have a lot of differences. Phobia is a serious disorder that can complicate life. It is often a sign of an anxiety disorder.

Many people experience anxiety at certain times. In children, social phobia can develop against the background of fear of learning. Some children are very afraid to answer in front of the whole class. In adults, fear can cause fear of speaking in front of a large audience, job interviews, communicating with new acquaintances, or visiting public institutions. The onset of unpleasant feelings may begin immediately before the terrifying event or a few days before.

Most people with this problem explain anxiety by fear of negative reactions: judgment, ridicule, and criticism. But they also try not to show their anxiety in public. As a result, a vicious circle is formed, as the fear of social phobia intensifies it even more.

This disorder does not lead to difficulty in socializing with all people. Many people with social phobia can communicate easily and at ease with their relatives and close friends.

However, socializing with unfamiliar people causes them serious difficulty and anxiety. If untreated, the disorder leads to permanent loneliness.

When people with social phobia are forced to participate in some kind of social interaction, he or she experiences increased anxiety, which negatively affects communication skills. As a result of constant psychological tension, he or she has problems with the formulation of thoughts, gestures, and facial expressions, which reduces the chances of pleasing people and making new acquaintances. People with these problems think that trying to avoid difficult situations will protect them from feelings of fear, but they only exacerbate the problem.

According to the results of numerous studies of human brain activity, people with social phobia have active work of the part of the brain responsible for emotions and feelings arising from uncomfortable and dangerous situations - the amygdala. Increased activity of this area contributes to the development of increased muscle tension, increased heart rate, and decreased brain and thinking capacity.

Social phobia, or social anxiety disorder, was indirectly by Hippocrates in the early 5th century BC. The ancient Greek philosopher was the first to figuratively articulate the feelings inherent in a person with social phobia: fear of being seen, fear that interaction with people is bound to lead to negative results - ridicule, insults, or even violence. Hippocrates called such emotions "shyness" - it was only later, at the turn of the 19th and 20th centuries, that Western psychiatric researchers suggested that such feelings, which encompass people, were more like a mental disorder and could be far more dangerous than mere shyness.

The terms "social phobia" and "social neurosis" were first mentioned by specialists in the early 20th century - they were to people with "extreme shyness". Nevertheless, a full understanding of what exactly social phobia consists of and how it manifests itself became possible only in the second half of the last century, after psychiatry had received the term "social phobia" and "social neurosis". after the method of systematic desensitization the psychiatrist Joseph Volpe's method of systematic desensitization became widespread. It's an approach that aims to This approach, which aims to reduce a person's emotional sensitivity in fearful situations, became the basis for cognitive behavioral therapy and, most importantly, allowed a deeper look at what a phobia is and how a person can overcome it.

Social phobia, according to various estimates, is "the third most common mental disorder" in the world: according to researchers, 7% of US residents have experienced it, and another 13% of Americans are at risk of developing it. In Europe, these figures are slightly (6.7% on average), and the lowest rates are recorded in China and Japan. In Russia, presumably, they may be even higher than in North America, at least, so by foreign researchers. What is interesting is that social phobia in different years and celebrities, whose lives are impossible without communication with the public. Among them are singers Barbra Streisand and Taylor Swift, TV presenter Oprah Winfrey, model Kourtney Kardashian, and actresses Whoopi Goldberg and Kristen Bell.

In terms of age, adolescents and young adults are most prone to social phobia. "There is a hypothesis that it is at this point that there is a kind of power struggle going on in social groups, which can include open aggression and even bullying. Social phobia in such a case would be a person's reaction to such violence, even if he or she is just acting as an observer," Laisheva explains. The causes of social phobia can also be other factors, such as genetic (according to the expert, there is a 30% probability that a parent's social phobia can be passed on to a child) or even congenital. In the latter case, it is a tendency to anxiety or increased emotional sensitivity, in which social contacts will be perceived more acutely.

Stages and forms of the disease

There are two types of social phobia:

Specific.
Anxiety occurs only in certain situations, but not in most situations. For example, when giving a speech in public or while singing/playing a musical instrument to a large audience, in the company of a particular person. The main symptoms include expectation of failure, anxiety, tremors, chills, and blushing. However, socializing with people outside of the frightening situation is not difficult.

Generalized.
Anxiety extends to all social interactions of a person. The generalized form of social phobia is characterized by the early onset of the disease (most often in childhood or adolescence), insufficient education of patients, and lack of work and family. In this case,

the patient feels pronounced fear, anxiety, and shame, being surrounded by other people. Common signs of generalized disorder include avoidant behavior, exclusion of any social contacts, and alienation from companies and society as a whole.

Usually, a person is initially haunted by intrusive thoughts that those around him will laugh at him, think badly of him, and insult him publicly. This condition is supplemented by other physiological symptoms. The result is a vicious circle: the person is afraid of developing social phobia, but due to the avoidance of social interaction, the disorder only intensifies and the symptoms become more pronounced.

Danger

If left untreated, social phobia persists throughout life and accompanies a person into adulthood.

The disorder affects all aspects of a person's life and leads to the following complications:

Development of other psychological disorders. Fear, anxiety, and isolation from society contribute to the development of such severe disorders as depression, panic attacks, generalized anxiety disorder, and obsessive-compulsive disorder.

Difficulties in getting an education and building a career. People with social phobia may avoid situations that require interacting with coworkers, teachers, or employers, which affects academic and work success.

Family problems. Because of avoidance of social contact and communication difficulties, patients often suffer from relationships with friends, family, and romantic partners.

Developing alcohol or drug dependence. Some people with social phobia resort to using alcohol or psychotropic substances to relieve symptoms.

Self-harm (self-harm). Patients with social phobia, due to low self-esteem and high demands on themselves in the face of setbacks and difficulties, may self-harm and even attempt suicide.

Signs of Social phobia

Social phobia can manifest itself mentally and physically. Signs occur directly when the fear-inducing factor is present or when thinking about it.

Psychological signs of social phobia include:

- Fear of certain moments (public events and speeches, communication with strangers, job interviews, negotiations, going to public places);
- fear of phone calls;
- low self-esteem;
- Increased irritability, anxiety, and excitability that occurs before interacting with people;
- inferiority complex;
- lack of confidence in their strengths and abilities;
- fear of losing control in public;
- a negative judgment of one's appearance;
- a tendency to be hypersensitive and resentful;
- constant anxiety;
- Fear of unexpected situations in public (loss of consciousness, disorientation in space, myocardial infarction).

In more serious forms of pathology, the patient may have suicidal thoughts.

Sociophobia can also manifest itself physically:

- a rise in blood pressure;
- tachycardia;
- violation of the rhythm and frequency of breathing, accompanied by shortness of breath;
- painful sensations in the chest area;
- a feeling of discomfort in the throat (feeling of a lump);
- hyperventilation of the lungs;
- neurasthenia;

- hyperhidrosis;
- flushes and facial redness;
- pain in the head;
- a feeling of nausea;
- tremors;
- abdominal discomfort;
- diarrhea;
- frequent urination;
- trouble sleeping.

When social phobia progresses, a person develops the habit of avoiding all stimuli. He begins to refuse any interaction with other people.

Causes of social phobia

The social disorder occurs against a background of various factors:

1. Hereditary predisposition. Most mental illnesses can be passed on from generation to generation.
2. Personality characteristics. Melancholics with an anxious-emotional psych type, prone to rapid fatigue or excitability, are more likely to suffer from increased anxiety and phobias.
3. Psychological trauma in childhood. Social phobia is often manifested in children and adolescents. It can be caused by insults in a public place, conflicts with other people, or poor social adaptation in kindergarten or school. Many people with social phobia have experienced humiliation and insults at school as children. They have not been able to get along well with other children.
4. Frequent stress. Constant stressful situations, exhaustion of the nervous system, and quarrels at work and home can trigger the development of a phobia.
5. Other neuropsychological disorders (neurosis, depressive state, episodic paroxysmal anxiety).
6. Drug and alcohol use. They disrupt the brain's neurotransmitter metabolism, which can result in increased anxiety, sleep problems, and nervousness.

Children can develop social phobia as a result of upbringing. If parents constantly overestimate the requirements for children's achievements and actions and do not support and treat them coldly, the child develops a fear of not living up to parental expectations. Also, anxiety occurs against the background of lack or excess of parental care and tutelage.

In adulthood, social phobia can be the cause of stress, serious deception, or violence (sexual or psychological).

Diagnosis

If you suspect a social disorder, you should see a psychotherapist. At the appointment, the therapist will conduct a detailed interview about your symptoms, feelings, thoughts, and social behavior. It is important to describe your experiences honestly and in detail so that the therapist can get a full picture of your condition. Recall the circumstances under which anxiety, fear, agitation, or panic attacks occur.

An important part of the consultation is taking a medical history. Tell the doctor about any family history of mental disorders (if any), previous treatments, and tests you have had. If you have been taking medications (e.g., antidepressants), remember their names and how long you have been taking them.

A psychotherapist can confirm the diagnosis if the patient's fear and anxiety have the following characteristics:

- distinct, lasting more than six months;
- are felt in the same social situation, or in different circumstances involving contact with people;
- almost always arise in a particular setting;
- characterized by fear of criticism and negative attitudes from others;
- lead to a person avoiding interaction with society;
- are not proportional to the actual danger;
- cause distress, and anxiety, interfere with work and relationships.

During the interview, the doctor will assess the severity of your symptoms and their impact on your daily life: interpersonal relationships, work, school, and leisure activities. The DSM-V classification of mental disorders is also used to confirm the diagnosis:

- Fear of one or more situations;
- A person's realization of the irrationality of their fear;
- Avoiding situations that seem dangerous and frightening;
- difficulties in daily life, work, or personal relationships due to anxious expectations of failure;
- excessive self-criticism, low self-esteem.

It is important to rule out other mental illnesses that have signs of social phobia: generalized anxiety disorder, depression, schizophrenia, and bipolar affective disorder. To do this, the doctor conducts additional tests and examinations.

After all examinations have been performed and the information gathered has been analyzed, the doctor will be able to diagnose social phobia if the symptoms meet its criteria. Further treatment plans may include psychotherapy (cognitive-behavioral therapy, psychoanalytic therapy), drug therapy, and other techniques. If the symptoms of social phobia are weakly expressed, a single consultation with a doctor is sufficient. In complex cases, long-term work with a psychotherapist is required, including several techniques.

Tests are often used to determine the severity of social phobia. The most common is the Liebowitz scale test. Based on their results, a preliminary diagnosis is made. Pathology is confirmed only if there are signs of it for several months.

Liebowitz Social Anxiety Scale testing

The method is designed to diagnose the level of social anxiety and its impact on adaptation in society.

Below you will find a description of 24 situations. You should give your answers based on the events of the past week up to and including today. You determine how anxious you were in the situation described, or would have been (if it had happened). You determine this using a 4-point system.

Also in the second column, indicate to what extent you avoid or would avoid these types of situations using a 4-point scale.

	Fear or anxiety	Situation avoidance
	1 = absent 2 = weakly expressed 3 = moderately pronounced 4 = strongly expressed	1 = never 2 = sometimes 3 = often 4 = usually
1. Talking on the phone in public places		
2. Participate in small group activities		
3. Eating in public places		
4. Drinking in public places		
5. Speaking to a superior (superior person)		
6. Performing any action or speaking in front of an audience		
7. Participate in a party, go out to visit		
8. To work under the supervision (presence) of someone.		
9. Writing under the supervision of (in the presence of) someone		
10. Talking on the phone with a stranger		
11. Talking face-to-face with a person you do not know well		
12. Meeting strangers		
13. Peeing in a public restroom.		
14. Entering a room where other people are already sitting.		
15. Being the center of attention		
16. Speaking at a meeting without preparation		
17. Test for skills, and knowledge abilities.		

18. Express disapproval or disagreement with a person you do not recognize		
19. Looking directly into the eyes of a stranger.		
20. Deliver a prepared speech to a group of people		
21. Trying to meet someone for a sexual or romantic relationship.		
22. Return the goods to the store or negotiate compensation.		
23. Organize a party / invite guests		
24. Resist the salesperson's persistent offers.		
Total Points:		
Summation:		

Count the sum of the points in the two columns.

Final Test Results:

55-65 - mild social phobia.

65-80 - quite pronounced social phobia.

80-95 - strong social phobia.

Over 95 - very strong social phobia.

Treatment

The following methods are used as the main methods:

- antidepressants, usually selective serotonin reuptake inhibitors (SSRIs);
- tranquilizers (are not a treatment, but only help to relieve symptoms for the first time);
- exposure therapy;
- cognitive behavioral therapy;
- psychotherapy using virtual reality technologies (VR-glasses).

Drug therapy

A psychotherapist may prescribe anxiolytics (tranquilizers) and antidepressants to alleviate the symptoms of social phobia. Anxiolytics can help reduce anxiety and reduce fear of social situations.

Specific drugs, dosages, and regimens are determined by the doctor after examination and history. If necessary, the treatment plan will have to be adjusted to achieve the best result. Drug therapy is most often used in combination with psychotherapeutic methods.

Psychotherapy

Exposure therapy is based on the gradual and controlled introduction of the patient to anxiety-provoking situations. In this way, the patient learns to overcome his or her fears. For example, people with social phobia who are afraid to engage in conversations with strangers may start with small steps: a simple greeting or neutral communication. Gradually, he or she moves on to more complex, distressing situations, such as communicating with coworkers, participating in discussions and meetings, and speaking in front of large audiences.

At the beginning of exposure therapy, patients may simply visualize or describe these situations. Gradually, they begin to actively engage in real social situations, learn to manage their emotions, and realize that their fears are not always justified. Exposure therapy helps patients reevaluate how they think and feel in social situations.

Cognitive behavioral therapy is a more widely used method of treating social phobia. It is based on the assumption that thoughts, feelings, and behaviors are interrelated and can be corrected through changes in thinking and behavior. In therapy, patients learn to recognize negative distorted thoughts that cause fear and anxiety. Cognitive-behavioral techniques help to reorganize thought patterns, change negative attitudes into positive ones, and stop associating situations with fear of failure, judgment, or ridicule from others.

VR-therapy also helps to overcome social phobia. With the help of VR-glasses and a special computer simulator program, a person is immersed in a virtual environment where he or she has to face his or her fears. The patient enters a thematic virtual space related to his phobia. At the same time, he feels safe, controls his behavior, and learns to overcome his fears. Sessions are supervised by an experienced psychotherapist, and during therapy, the doctor determines the level of anxiety on a 10-point scale.

VR-therapy is also effective for other phobias that often accompany social phobia - anthropophobia (fear of people) agoraphobia (fear of open spaces), pediophobia (fear of dolls), and others.

A combined approach, including both psychotherapeutic methods (exposure, cognitive-behavioral, or hypnotherapy) and medications, is often most effective. An individualized treatment plan is selected depending on the severity of symptoms, the patient's preferences, and medical indications.

Techniques for CBT work with social phobia

However, a specialist or the necessary medication may not always be available, and it is not uncommon to have to cope with social phobia on one's own. In such situations, psychologists use the **"five senses" technique:** when in a stressful situation, a person with social anxiety is advised to focus on what he or she sees, hears, feels with body parts, etc. This approach helps to concentrate solely on one's sensations and to distract oneself from thoughts of being watched, judged, or evaluated, in other words, the most disturbing thoughts of a person with social phobia.

If the symptoms of social anxiety come on suddenly, to cope If the symptoms of social anxiety are sudden, a breathing practice that can be repeated in a circle until the discomfort subsides can help:

1. sit in a comfortable position with your back straight;
2. relax your shoulders;
3. put one hand on your stomach and the other on your chest;
4. take slow nose breaths - focus on how the hand on your stomach rises and the hand on your chest, on the contrary, remains stationary;
5. hold your breath for two seconds, and then for another six, exhale.

Let's talk some more about cognitive techniques that aim to correct dysfunctional thoughts and beliefs.

The first technique focuses on tracking and recognizing your unconstructive thoughts. This step is the most crucial and the most time-consuming. Why do you ask? Recognizing the problem in some cases leads to healing, and sometimes it provides an accurate map of actions without which it would be impossible to move towards healing.

We have already talked about the Events-My Thoughts-Emotions-Reactions technique. Its essence is to track what events and thoughts lead to what emotions and reactions.

Such tracking gives you a better understanding of yourself, plus you train yourself to observe your body, thoughts, and emotions. This exercise is usually recommended for a few days, but I would recommend writing out at least 1-3 strong emotions a day for a month without weekends and without skipping. And if you miss a long time, start from the beginning. It's a free but so effective tool. The most important thing is your motivation. In the psychologist's office, you will be offered to do similar homework, but you will pay for it.

Here is an example of a diary that you can keep for yourself and work on understanding the causes of certain emotions:

Event	Thoughts	Emotions	Reactions	
			Body	**Behavior**

The second method is Distancing.

It is explained to the person what automatic thoughts are, and that these thoughts are reflexively triggered by the situation and related only to it. In various other circumstances, that thought would no longer be functional. For example, if I experience anxiety in the boss's office, it doesn't mean that next time it will be too. It learns to assess the credibility of that dysfunctional thought and find - a thought alternative that it will trust more. At the expense of this, substitution occurs.

Another technique is aimed at teaching the person to challenge these maladaptive automatic thoughts. He is asked to evaluate these thoughts using the "pros and cons" technique to understand whether they are illusory or realistic. For example, a person is the best worker in a department but is constantly afraid of being fired and is asked to evaluate the facts, what is in favor of this and what is not.

Another technique is called "advantages and disadvantages," which assesses decisions and behavior. For example, asking a girl to choose whether to be wary of pursuing relationships with men after a failure or to try again.

The next technique is talking to witnesses of past events or an experiment. For example, if a person believes that someone is angry with them, it is suggested that they begin by simply asking that person "Is this true?".

Well, one of the most powerful, techniques "Socratic dialog", using which the therapist checks logical errors in the client's reasoning.

For example, a person states that he may die from a spider bite, although he has previously stated that a spider bit him and he did not die. The therapist might point this out to him. This is a crude example, but the point is this.

The decatastrophizing technique, the point of it is to develop the client's thoughts to devalue them.

For example, a client is afraid to enter the subway, and the therapist asks,

"What happens if you go down to the subway?

The client responds, "I'm going to be sick and I'm going to choke."

The therapist asks what happens next.

The client responds with "I'm going to feel bad and stuff."

The therapist asks by "unpacking" the client's fears to get to the finale.

"What happens next, do you die, or what happens to you?"

That is, sooner or later, in this process, the client, begins to realize the absurdity and will say that he has never died yet and thus the automatic thought is devalued.

Here are some of the best tools from CBT for working with social phobia. I have put them all in a table that you can use. My recommendation is to practice, no cognitive behavioral therapy exercise or any other will work if you don't use them. To understand this tool, this technique will help you or not, you have to try it at least once. So, let's take a look at our table:

1	**Exploring and recognizing irrational beliefs**	The first step in overcoming social phobia is recognizing and understanding the irrational beliefs that underlie it. These may be thoughts that others are judging you or not accepting you, or beliefs that you are unable to hold a conversation or be interesting to others.
2	**Challenging and replacing irrational beliefs**	Use CBT techniques to challenge and replace irrational beliefs with more sensible and realistic ones. This may include asking yourself questions such as, "What evidence do I have to support this belief?" or "What are alternative explanations for this situation?
3	**Exposure and desensitization**	These CBT techniques help people gradually become accustomed to frightening situations. Exposure involves gradual exposure to social situations, starting with less frightening ones and gradually progressing to more frightening ones. Desensitization combines exposure to frightening situations with relaxation techniques to help soothe anxiety reactions.
4	**Overcoming perfectionism**	Many people with social phobia have idealized expectations of themselves in social situations. Examining and challenging these beliefs, and practicing accepting oneself with fewer demands and expectations, can help reduce anxiety and stress.
5	**Practicing social communication skills**	Developing effective communication skills and confidence in social situations is a key aspect of overcoming social phobia. Practicing listening and active communication can help improve communication skills and self-esteem.
	Self-help and support	Include taking care of your physical and emotional well-being, such as healthy living, stress management, and self-care. Getting support from family, friends, or professional therapists can also help overcome social phobia.

Overcoming social phobia can be a challenge, but with effective tools from CBT and ongoing practice, you can develop healthier strategies for coping with your fears and improve your quality of life. Remember that each coping process is different, and it is important to find an approach that fits your needs and characteristics.

Psychologists insist: that despite your fear, you should not give up on social interactions even when they seem very unpleasant. Fighting your fear and overcoming it in this way is essential, and the most effective way is to do so, by adding to your daily life with helpful therapeutic practices. One of these is keeping a diary in which you can note successes and failures and record your feelings about each social interaction with people.

The usual things such as regular healthy lifestyles (exercise, avoid alcohol, eat a balanced diet) and setting clear goals that one would like to achieve in the foreseeable future can also help to cope with social phobia. These could be, for example, performing just the social interactions themselves, whether it's making a phone call, participating in a videoconference, or giving a presentation. For each successful step in the fight against fear, experts recommend praising yourself, because a person with social phobia finds it more difficult to communicate than others, and even a step of little importance in the eyes of society can have a huge impact on him.

Prevention

There are no specific preventive measures. It is possible to prevent the development of the disorder by taking care of mental health from childhood and using cognitive-behavioral therapy.

Primary prevention includes:

1. Increased attention to the upbringing of children. From childhood, encourage your child to develop social skills, help them learn to communicate with others, resolve conflicts, and cope with unpleasant situations.
2. Improving stress resilience. Learn to manage your emotions and overcome anxiety. Breathing exercises, relaxation, and meditation practices often help.
3. Work on self-esteem. Building confidence will help make you less vulnerable to the fear of evaluation and judgment.

Secondary prevention is necessary if the disorder has already been diagnosed. It helps to reduce the likelihood of recurrence of the disease and makes life easier for a person with social phobia. The main recommendations:

- regular psychotherapy sessions;
- Compliance with doctor's recommendations, such as taking antidepressants as prescribed;
- avoiding bad habits;
- support of social relations - active participation in social networks, training, and discussions.

Forecast

If left untreated, sociophobe people remain anxious and tension builds up. The quality of life deteriorates due to a decrease in social skills. Problems in professional activity, personal life, and everyday life often lead to complete isolation.

If you suspect social phobia, you should not delay with a visit to a specialist. It is best to consult a psychotherapist at the initial stage when the phobia has just appeared and does not yet affect all areas of life. If you seek medical help promptly, the prognosis of the social disorder is quite favorable.

The total duration of treatment, depending on the severity and duration of social phobia, can range from 2-3 months to a year or more. The prognosis in most cases is favorable. With adequate therapy, a high level of motivation, and active participation of the socio-phobic patient in the psychotherapeutic process, a complete cure is possible. Prognostically unfavorable signs are late treatment, severe social disadaptation, a combination of social phobia with other mental disorders, alcoholism, and drug addiction.

Conclusion

Glad to welcome you at the end of the road. I hope you found the information in this book useful. As a summary, I invite you to answer the following questions for yourself to help you take stock and determine what tools you will use to work on yourself in the future.

Please take the time and quiet space to work on the following questions:

What was helpful:

_____

_____

_____

What new things have you learned:

_____

_____

_____

What you learned about yourself:

_____

_____

_____

What knowledge you will take with you:

_____

_____

_____

What knowledge do you think will be useful to you in the future:

_____

_____

_____

What knowledge do you want to share with others:

_____

_____

_____

References

1. In Ribbens, J. and Edwards, R. (eds.), Feminist Dilemmas in Qualitative Research. London: Sage Publications (pp. 147–70).

2. Althusser, L. (1977). For Marx. London: New Left Books.

3. Alvarez, A. (1992). Live Company: Psychoanalytic Psychotherapy with Autistic, Borderline, Deprived and Abused Children. London: Routledge.

4. Ardener, E. (1971a). Introductory Essay: Social Anthropology and Language.

5. Asch, S. E. (1955). Opinions and Social Pressure. Scientific American, 193, 31–5.

6. Aspect, A., Dalibard, J. and Roger, G. (1982). Experimental Test of Bell's Inequalities Using Time-Varying Analyzers. Physical Review Letters, 39, 1804–7.

7. Aurelius, M. (c. 170). Meditations. Harmondsworth: Penguin Books (this version was published in 1964).

8. Austin, J. (1962). How To Do Things with Words. Cambridge, MA: Harvard University Press (1975).

9. Australian Psychological Society (1997). What is Clinical Psychology? Melbourne: Australian Psychological Society.

10. Australian Psychological Society (2002). APS Accreditation Guidelines. Melbourne: Australian Psychological Society.

11. Baddeley, A. D. (1989). Human Memory: Theory and Practice. Hillsdale, NJ: Lawrence Erlbaum.

12. Bak, P. (1997). How Nature Works: The Science of Self-Organized Criticality. Oxford: Oxford University Press.

13. Bakhtin, M. M. (1986). Speech Genres and Other Late Essays (McGee, V. W., trans.). Austin: University of Texas Press. (Original work published 1979.).

14. Baldwin, J. M. (1895). Mental Development in the Child and the Race: Methods and Processes. New York: Macmillan and Co.

15. Bales, R. F. and Strodtbeck, F. L. (1951). Phases in Group Problem-Solving. Journal of Abnormal and Social Psychology, 46, 385–95.

16. Bayer, B. M. and Shotter, J. (eds.) (1998). Reconstructing the Psychological Subject: Bodies, Practices and Technologies. London: Sage.

17. Bernstein, N. (1967). The Coordination and Regulation of Movements. Oxford: Pergamon.

18. Billig, M. (2003). Towards a Critical View of Humour. Keynote Address Delivered at the International Conference of Critical Psychology, University of Bath, Friday 29th August.

19. Bradley, B. S. (1981). Negativity in Early Infant–Adult Exchanges and its Developmental Significance. In Robinson, W. P. (ed.), Communication in Development. London: Academic (pp. 153–61).

20. Bradley, B. S. (1991). Infancy as Paradise. Human Development, 34, 35–54.

21. Bradley, B. S. (1993a). A Serpent's Guide to Children's 'Theories of Mind'. Theory and Psychology, 3, 497–521.

22. Bradley, B. S. and Trevarthen, C. (1978). Babytalk as an Adaptation to the Infant's Communication. In Waterson, N. and Snow, C. (eds.), The Development of Communication. Chichester: Wiley (pp. 75–92).

23. Braungert-Rieker, J. M., Garwood, M. M., Powers, B. P. and Wang, X. (2001). Parental Sensitivity, Infant Affect, and Affect Regulation: Predictors of Later Attachment. Child Development, 72, 252–70.

24. Brown, L. M. and Gilligan, C. (1993). Meeting at the Crossroads: Women's Psychology and Girl's Development. Cambridge, MA: Harvard University Press.

25. Bruner, J. S., (1974). Beyond the Information Given: Studies in the Psychology of Knowing. London: Allen and Unwin.

26. Bruner, J. S. (1975). The Ontogenesis of Speech Acts. Journal of Child Language, 2, 1–19.

27. Buber, M., (1970). I and Thou. New York: Scribner.

28. Bullowa, M. (ed.) (1979). Before Speech: The Beginnings of Human Communication. Cambridge: Cambridge University Press.

29. Butler, S. (1879). Evolution Old and New: Or Theories of Buffon, Dr. Erasmus Darwin, and Lamarck as Compared with that of Mr. Charles Darwin. London: Hardwicke and Bogue.

30. Butler, S. (1880). Unconscious Memory: A Comparison between the Theory of Dr. Ewald Hering and 'The Philosophy of the Unconscious' of Dr. Edward von Hartmann; With Translations from these Authors, and Preliminary Chapters Bearing on 'Life and Habit', 'Evolution, Old and New', and Mr. Charles Darwin's Edition of Dr. Krause's 'Erasmus Darwin'. London: Bogue.

31. Cahan, E. D. and White, S. H. (1992). Proposals for a Second Psychology. American Psychologist, 47, 224–35.

32. Campbell, D. T. and Stanley, J. C. (1966). Experimental and Quasi-Experimental Designs for Research. Boston: Houghton-Mifflin.

33. Chasin, R. and Herzig, M. (1992). Creating Systemic Interventions for the Sociopolitical Arena. In Berger-Could, B. and DeMuth, D. H. (eds.), The Global Family Therapist: Integrating the Personal, Professional, and Political. Needham, MA: Allyn and Bacon (pp. 141–92).

34. Claxton, G. (ed.) (1980). Cognitive Psychology: New Directions. London: Routledge and Kegan Paul.

35. Coles, R. (1986). Children of Crisis: A Study of Courage and Fear, vol. I. London: Faber and Faber.

36. Courtenay, W. H. (1998). Better to Die than Cry? A Longitudinal and Constructionist Study of Masculinity and the Health Risk Behaviour of Young American Men. PhD thesis, University of California at Berkeley.

37. Cowan, N. (1997). Attention and Memory: An Integrated Framework. New York: Oxford University Press.

38. Craik, J. (1994). The Face of Fashion: Cultural Studies in Fashion. London: Routledge.

39. Critchley, S. (1999). Ethics Politics Subjectivity: Essays on Derrida, Levinas and Contemporary French Thought. London: Verso.

40. Crossley, N. (1996). Intersubjectivity: The Fabric of Social Becoming. London: Sage.

41. Csikszentmihalyi, M. (1990). Flow: The Psychology of Optimal Experience. New York: Harper and Row.

42. Danziger, K. (1997). Naming the Mind: How Psychology Found its Language. London: Sage Publications.

43. Darwin, C. R. (1871). The Descent of Man and Selection in Relation to Sex. London: Murray (this version published in 1901).

44. Darwin, C. R. (1958). The Autobiography of Charles Darwin, 1809–1882. With Original Omissions Restored (Barlow, N., ed.). London: Collins.

45. Darwin, E. (1803). The Temple of Nature or the Origin of Society: A Poem with Philosophical Notes. London: Johnson.

46. Dawes, R. M. (1996). House of Cards: Psychology and Psychotherapy Built on Myth. New York: Free Press.

47. Derrida, J. (1967). Freud and the Scene of Writing. In Meisel, P. (ed.), Freud: A Collection of Critical Essays. Englewood Cliffs, NJ: Prentice-Hall (this version published in 1981, pp. 145–82).

48. Devereux, G. (1968). From Anxiety to Method in the Behavioural

49. Donald, M. (2001). A Mind so Rare: The Evolution of Human Edelman, G. M., (1988). Topobiology: An Introduction to Molecular Embryology. New York: Basic Books.

50. Fairweather, G. W. (1979). Experimental Development and Dissemination of an Alternative to Psychiatric Hospitalization: Scientific Methods for Social Change. In Munoz, R. F., Snowden, L. R., Kelly, J. G. and Associates (eds.), Social and Psychological Research in Community Settings. San Fransisco: Jossey-Bass (pp. 305–26).

51. Falk, R. (1982). On Coincidences. The Skeptical Inquirer, 6, 18–31.

52. Festinger, L. and Carlsmith, J. M. (1959). Cognitive Consequences of Forced Compliance. Journal of Abnormal and Social Psychology, 58, 203–10.

53. Franklin, J. (1998). Introduction. In Franklin, J. (ed.), The Politics of Risk Society. Cambridge: Polity Press (pp. 1–8).

54. Fraser, N., (1989). Unruly Practices: Power, Discourse and Gender in Contemporary Social Theory. Cambridge: Polity Press.

55. Gard, M. and Bradley, B. S. (2000). Getting Away with Rape: Erasure of the Psyche in Evolutionary Psychology. Psychology, Evolution and Gender, 2, 313–19.

56. Gergen, K. J. (1999). An Invitation to Social Constructionism. London.

57. Ghaye, T. and Lillyman, S. (eds.) (2000). Caring Moments: The Discourse of Reflective Practice. Dinton, UK: Quay Books.

58. Stoppard, J. (2000). Navigating the Hazards of Orthodoxy: Introducing a Graduate Course on Qualitative Methods into the Psychology Curriculum. Canadian Psychology, 43, 143–53.

59. Tanner, C. and Jungbluth, N. (2003). Evidence for the Coincidence Effect in Environmental Judgments: Why Isn't It Easy to Correctly Identify Environmentally Friendly Food Products? Journal of Experimental Psychology: Applied, 9, 3–11.

60. Tooby, J. and Cosmides, L. (1990). The Past Explains the Present: Emotional Adaptations and the Structure of Ancestral Environments. Ethology and Sociobiology, 11, 375–424.

61. Trevarthen, C. B. (1979). Communication and Cooperation in Early Infancy: A Description of Primary Intersubjectivity. In Bullowa (ed.), pp. 321–47.

62. Trevarthen, C. B. (2000). Musicality and the Intrinsic Motive Pulse: Evidence from Human Tsien, J. Z. (2000). Linking Hebb's coincidence-detection to memory formation. Current Opinion in Neurobiology, 10, 266–73.

A Special Gift for You, Dear Reader!

As a token of my gratitude for choosing this book, I am thrilled to offer you an exclusive bonus – the complete audio version of this book!

Whether you're on the go or prefer to listen while relaxing, the audio recording enhances your experience. Simply scan the QR code with your phone, and you'll be directed to the audio file stored on Dropbox. Just point, scan, and enjoy!

Thank you for being part of this journey. Happy listening!

Made in the USA
Middletown, DE
19 November 2024

64986561R00084